THE RAF

IN CAMERA

ALSO BY ROY CONYERS NESBIT

Woe to the Unwary

Torpedo Airmen

The Strike Wings

Target: Hitler's Oil (with Ron C. Cooke)

Arctic Airmen (with Ernest Schofield)

Failed to Return

An Illustrated History of the RAF

RAF Records in the PRO (with Simon Fowler, Peter Elliott and Christina Goulter)

The Armed Rovers

THE RAF
IN CAMERA

ARCHIVE PHOTOGRAPHS FROM THE PUBLIC RECORD OFFICE
AND THE MINISTRY OF DEFENCE

1903–1939

ROY CONYERS NESBIT

Assisted by Oliver Hoare

ALAN SUTTON PUBLISHING LIMITED
IN ASSOCIATION WITH THE PUBLIC RECORD OFFICE

First published in the United Kingdom in 1995 by
Alan Sutton Publishing Ltd · Phoenix Mill · Far Thrupp · Stroud · Gloucestershire
in association with the Public Record Office

British Library Cataloguing in Publication Data

A catalogue record for this book is available from the British Library.

ISBN 0-7509-1054-2

Typeset in 11/15pt Baskerville.
Typesetting and origination by
Alan Sutton Publishing Limited.
Printed in Great Britain by
Butler & Tanner, Frome, Somerset.

CONTENTS

INTRODUCTION

For many years numerous photographs relating to the activities of the RAF have remained unrecorded in hundreds of documents in the Public Record Office in Kew. Another large collection is housed in the Ministry of Defence in London. This series of three volumes is intended to bring representative photographs of the two collections to the notice of the general public. The volumes are not intended to provide a comprehensive history of the RAF and its predecessors, but they may give some indication of the huge numbers of photographs which are available.

In all cases the reference numbers of the photographs appear underneath the captions. The photographs at the PRO (Ruskin Avenue, Richmond, Kew, Surrey TW9 4DU) are not housed separately but the originals of each may be seen within their relevant documents by visitors who obtain readers' tickets and then request the numbers on computer terminals in the Reference Room. However, it should be noted that no documents at the PRO are available for public scrutiny until they are thirty years old, and the same stipulation normally applies to photographs.

A catalogue of many photographs of all types at the PRO has been built up and is available in the Reference Room, but at the time of writing this is by no means complete. A description of the contents of this catalogue is contained in PRO leaflet Number Ninety. Copies of RAF photographs, or any others found by readers, may be purchased via the Reprographic Department. Details such as choice of process and scale of charges are set out in PRO leaflet Number Nineteen.

The photographic prints relating to the RAF which are housed at the Ministry of Defence are not available for public inspection. The main purpose of this collection is to provide information to the RAF and various Government departments, and not to the general public. However, readers may write to the central library where negatives are held if they wish to purchase copies of the photographs contained in these volumes or enquire about others. This is CS(Photography)P, Ministry of Defence, Court 9 Basement, King Charles Street, London SW1A 2AH, with whom any purchasing arrangements may be made. At present the prints housed at the Ministry of Defence cover the period from the very early days of the RAF and its predecessors up to the Gulf War of 1991.

Photographs in all three volumes are Crown Copyright. Guidelines for those who propose to reproduce photographs are set out in PRO leaflet Number Fifteen, and the same guidelines also apply to any photographs purchased from the MoD.

This volume is the first of the series of three. It begins in 1903, when the Balloon Sections of the Royal Engineers were beginning to develop an interest in the military possibilities of powered flight. It continues with the formation of the Royal Flying Corps on 13 April 1912 and the Royal Naval Air Service on 1 July 1914, and the outbreak of the First World War on 4 August 1914. Photographs of the campaigns on the Western Front, the Dardanelles and the Middle East are included. This period also covers the formation of the Royal Air Force on 1 April 1918. There are photographs showing the effects of the German bombing in Britain and those of the RAF on Germany and German-held territory, including those of the RAF's Independent Force formed on 6 June 1918. The interwar photographs cover the rapid reduction of the RAF after the First World War and its reconstitution following the discovery that it was a potent instrument for controlling countries of the British Empire. It ends with the development of new aircraft and expansion up to the outbreak of the Second World War, including the formation of Bomber Command, Fighter Command, Coastal Command and Training Command in 1936.

The choice of photographs depended partly on their clarity, while the available space in the book did not permit the inclusion of every activity of the RAF or every aircraft flown by its units. The captions underneath these photographs originated from the documents in which they were located in the PRO or the brief captions available in the Ministry of Defence. This information was supplemented by a considerable amount of research in other documents in the PRO or reliable books of reference. Readers who wish to carry out similar research are recommended to purchase a copy of *RAF Records in the PRO* (PRO Reader's Guide Number Eight), published in 1994 at £8.95 and available from the PRO Shop. This guide also includes an Appendix listing other sources of RAF photographs within Great Britain.

Note   PRO leaflets are constantly being updated and their reference numbers are therefore liable to change from time to time.

ACKNOWLEDGEMENTS

I should like to express my gratitude to Oliver Hoare and Simon Fowler of the PRO for their painstaking help in hunting for suitable photographs and also to Mark Laing of Indusfoto for photographic work. Similarly, I am most grateful to Group Captain Ian Madelin RAF (Ret'd) and Squadron Leader Peter Singleton RAF (Ret'd) of the Air Historical Branch (RAF), Ministry of Defence, for permission to include many official photographs housed in the MoD, as well as to Bill Hunt of the Whitehall Library for producing the prints. My thanks for researching the material for captions are also due to Richard Riding, Michael Oakey and Phil Jarrett of *Aeroplane Monthly*, as well as Rick Chapman of the German aviation magazine *Jet & Prop*. I am extremely grateful to Squadron Leader Dudley Cowderoy RAFVR, Roger Hayward and Richard King for their work in checking and correcting the lengthy captions. Any errors which remain after all this expertise are my own responsibility.

HESITANT BEGINNINGS

On 13 March 1903 experiments with a man-carrying kite, developed by the American Samuel F. Cody, took place on Woolwich Common. Cody, shown here wearing his large hat, was employed by the War Office to experiment with kites as alternatives to balloons for observation purposes. Balloons had been used with advantage by the British Army during the Boer War, but in those days they were circular and spun round in the air. They also became targets for enemy gunners, since they took a long time to inflate, launch, bring back to earth and deflate, before the balloon team could load them on to horse carriages and gallop away out of range.

PRO ref: CN 1/24

Samuel F. Cody in the air. He ascended to about 200 feet, but far greater altitudes were later achieved.
PRO ref: CN 1/24

Further experiments with the Cody kite took place from HMS *Vernon* and Whale Island at Portsmouth on 4 April 1903.

PRO ref: CN 1/24

Between September and November 1904 Lieutenant-Colonel John E. Capper, the Officer Commanding the Balloon Sections of the Royal Engineers, visited the Louisiana Purchase Exposition at St Louis on behalf of the War Office. One of the photographs he brought back showed this model made by Samuel Pierpont Langley, the distinguished Third Secretary of the Smithsonian Institution, who devoted the last twenty years of his life to aeronautics. Langley's machine failed to fly, largely because he could not find an engine light enough for the airframes, and his efforts were held up to ridicule. However, before his death in 1906 his researches were justified when the first flight was made on 14 December 1903 by Wilbur Wright in *Flyer I* near Kitty Hawk in North Carolina, after the Wright brothers had built their own engine.

PRO ref: AIR 1/728/176/3/17/17a

Other photographs brought back by Lt.-Col. J.E. Capper from the Louisiana Purchase Exposition showed a Chanute glider. Octave Chanute, an engineer born in France but educated in America, began experiments with gliders in 1896 when he was over sixty years of age.

PRO ref: AIR 1/728/176/3/17/17a

The Chanute glider in the air. Octave Chanute collaborated with Wilbur and Orville Wright in experimenting with methods of controlling gliders in flight, some of the results being incorporated in the Wright brothers' *Flyer I*.
PRO ref: AIR 1/728/176/3/17/17a

The British Army airship *Nulli Secundus 1* was built in 1907 at the Army Balloon Factory at Farnborough. It was a semi-rigid airship with a length of 122 feet and a volume of 55,000 cubic feet, powered by an Antoinette engine of 50 hp. On 5 October 1907 the airship flew from Aldershot to the Crystal Palace, much to the fascination of the British public.

PRO ref: AIR 1/729/176/5/50

On 9 January 1909 the American aviator Samuel F. Cody took off from Farnborough Common in *British Army Aeroplane No. 1* for a short hop of 60 feet. The machine was powered by the 50 hp Antoinette engine, which had been used in the airship *Nulli Secundus 1*, and had been reconstructed after making its first flights during the previous year. On this occasion the aircraft carried a Union Jack as well as ribbon streamers attached to the airframe, so that the effect of the airflow could be observed.

PRO ref: AIR 1/729/176/5/58

The Army airship *Gamma* was completed in February 1910, rebuilt from *Nulli Secundus 2*. She was non-rigid, with a length of 160 feet and a volume of 72,000 cubic feet, and powered by a Green engine of 80 hp. In 1912 she was rebuilt once more, when two 45 hp engines were fitted and the volume increased to 101,000 cubic feet. She was broken up shortly before the First World War.

PRO ref: AIR 1/728/176/3/38

The two-seat Blériot monoplane *Le Scarabée*, in which Jacques de Lesseps made the second Channel crossing on 21 May 1910. He won the Ruinart Prize for the first crossing since Louis Blériot, who crossed on 25 July 1909, failed to make a formal entry for the prize. De Lesseps landed on a field at St Margaret's Bay in Kent, where this photograph was taken.

PRO ref: COPY 1/545

The Bristol Boxkite, powered by a Gnôme engine of 50 hp, was a successful biplane. Several were built in 1910 and the one in this photograph was demonstrated on 21 September by Captain Bertram Dickson during British Army manoeuvres held on Salisbury Plain. These were attended by Lord Kitchener, Lord Roberts, Sir John French and the Home Secretary, Winston Churchill.

PRO ref: AIR 1/7/6/98/3

Capt. Bertram Dickson returning from reconnaissance in his Bristol Boxkite during Army manoeuvres on 21 September 1910. Five days later a successful wireless transmission from one of these machines was achieved over Salisbury Plain.

PRO ref: AIR 1/7/6/98/4

This Paulhan biplane, fitted with a Gnôme engine of 50 hp, was photographed at Manchester on 28 April 1910, after the Frenchman Louis Paulhan had won a *Daily Mail* prize of £10,000 by completing the first flight from London to Manchester. The design of the aircraft was considered unusual since the ends of curved ribs, attached to spars, were slid into pockets of the fabric of the wings, rudder and tailplane.

PRO ref: COPY 1/545

A Short-Wright biplane, one of six built by the company with various engines, owned by Cecil S. Grace in early 1910. In one of these machines the Hon. Charles S. Rolls of Rolls-Royce made the first return flight across the Channel without landing, on 2 June 1910.

PRO ref: COPY 1/545

Cecil S. Grace in his Short-Wright biplane. He disappeared on 22 December 1910 while attempting to cross the Channel in a Short S27.

PRO ref: COPY 1/545

Frenchman Pierre Prier in the cockpit of his Blériot monoplane, fitted with a Gnôme engine of 50 hp, in which he flew non-stop from London to Issy-les-Moulineaux, near Paris, on 12 April 1911. The panel was fitted with a roll-map and two instruments, while by his right knee was a pulsometer to indicate fuel. Prier was the chief instructor at the Blériot School at Hendon.

PRO ref: COPY 1/556

A Blériot monoplane with a 80 hp engine being flown over Burnham on 16 August 1911 by the demonstration pilot B.C. Bucks (printed in error on the photograph as Hucks). On the outbreak of war three Blériot monoplanes owned by 2nd Lieutenant Bucks of the RFC were pressed into service and he was allocated one of his own machines, which was given the serial number 619.

PRO ref: COPY 1/565

HM Airship *Beta 2* was non-rigid, built from *Beta 1* which was damaged in 1911. Her length was 108 feet, the volume 35,000 cubic feet, and she was powered by a Clerget engine of 50 hp. She flew with the Royal Navy at the beginning of the First World War before being scrapped.

PRO ref: AIR 1/729/176/3/38

This Vickers Naval Rigid Airship No. 1, 512 feet long and 48 feet wide, was aptly named *Mayfly* before being launched from her shed at Barrow-in-Furness on 22 May 1911. Work continued but she was destined never to fly, breaking her back at her mooring mast on 24 September 1911, as shown in this photograph.

PRO ref: AIR 1/7/6/98/15

On 22 July 1911 a Circuit of Britain air race began, following an offer by the *Daily Mail* of a prize of £10,000 to the winner. Twenty-one aircraft were ready for the start at Brooklands. The route of 1,010 miles took the competitors on a flight of at least five days to Hendon, Harrogate, Newcastle, Edinburgh, Glasgow, Manchester, Bristol, Exeter, Salisbury and Brighton, ending at Brooklands. This photograph of a Deperdussin monoplane flown by James Valentine was taken at Bristol.

PRO ref: COPY 1/559

The winner on 26 July 1911 of the Circuit of Britain air race was *Lt. de Vaisseau* Conneau in a Blériot monoplane, with E. Véndrines in a Morane-Borel monoplane taking second place. James Valentine (shown here) took the third place, running a day behind these two Frenchmen.

PRO ref: COPY 1/559

The first trials of a British seaplane took place in 1911 when an Avro D biplane, powered by a Green engine of 35 hp, was fitted with floats made by the Royal Navy. The machine was taken to Cavendish Dock, Barrow-in-Furness. After several unsuccessful attempts, it rose about twenty feet above the sea on 18 November 1911. Although damaged on landing, this was the first British aircraft to take off from water. When fitted with redesigned floats, the machine was more successful in the following year.

PRO ref: AIR 1/7/6/1

The RFC experimented with a number of Deperdussin monoplanes after its formation on 13 April 1912. When a number of monoplanes of this type crashed and caused fatalities, the War Office effectively banned further experiments and ensured that designs concentrated on the stable biplanes with which RFC and RNAS squadrons were equipped at the outbreak of the First World War. This Deperdussin was crewed by C.F. Webb in the front cockpit and W.T.J. McCudden in the rear. McCudden later achieved fame as one of Britain's most successful fighter pilots.

MoD ref: B1905

The original Royal Aircraft Factory FE1 (Farman or Fighter Experimental 1), designed by Geoffrey de Havilland and fitted with an Iris pusher engine of 45 hp, first flew in January 1911 but crashed the following summer. It was rebuilt in September 1911, with a Gnôme engine of 50 hp and several other changes, and was redesignated the FE2. Rebuilt once more with a Renault engine of 70 hp, the FE2 flew in August 1913, as shown in this photograph.

PRO ref: AIR 1/2411/303/4/20

The rebuilt Royal Aircraft Factory FE2, photographed on 24 September 1913 at the Royal Aircraft Establishment, Farnborough.

PRO ref: AIR 1/729/176/5/27

This Royal Aircraft Factory FE3 was built in 1913 as an experimental machine, with a Chenu engine of 80 hp and a Coventry Ordnance Works one-pounder gun firing through the nose. The gun was never fired in the air, but only when the machine was suspended by ropes from a gantry. The machine was not put into production.

PRO ref: AIR 1/2411/303/4/20

The Royal Aircraft Factory RE1 (Reconnaissance Experimental) was built in 1913 as an improvement on the BE (Blériot Experimental) design. It was a two-seater aircraft with a tractor engine. Only serials 607 and 608 were built and the design did not go into general production. One RE1, fitted with a Renault engine of 70 hp, served with the RFC's 2 Squadron on the Western Front. This photograph was taken when the RE1 was undergoing tests on the upper and lower mainplanes with packages of sand totalling 4,000 lb.

PRO ref: AIR 1/2411/303/4/20

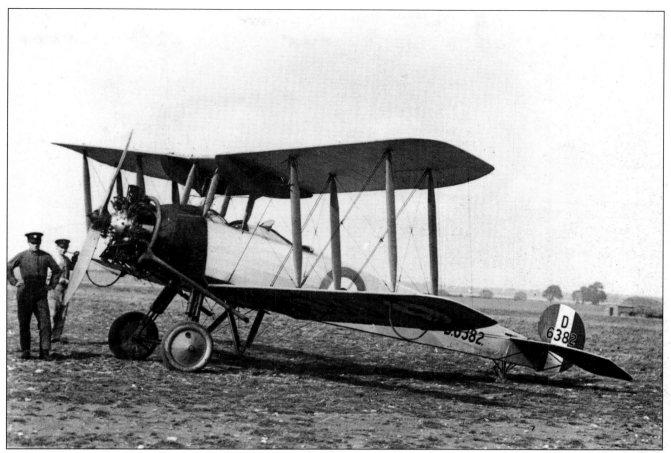

The career of the Avro 504 spanned two decades following its appearance in 1913 as a two-seat reconnaissance aircraft. Several of these aircraft, fitted with 80 hp Gnôme engines, saw service with the RFC and RNAS on the Western Front in the early months of the war. There were several variants of the Avro 504. Some were employed on home defence but the aircraft is best remembered as a reliable trainer, a role in which it continued until the 1930s, by which time over 10,000 had been built. This Avro 504N serial D6382 was subcontracted to the Brush Engineering Co. Ltd at Loughborough, and was converted from a 504K by fitting an Armstrong Siddeley Lynx engine. It was on the strength of No. 2 Flying Training School at Digby in Lincolnshire in the 1920s and was still flying in February 1933.

MoD ref: H1632

The Royal Aircraft Factory BE2 (Blériot Experimental) was a two-seat reconnaissance aircraft with a 70 hp Renault engine, designed by Geoffrey de Havilland, which first appeared in 1912. This photograph was taken at Farnborough on 24 January 1913, with Wingfield Smith in the cockpit.

PRO ref: AIR 1/729/176/5/38

This Royal Aircraft Factory BE3 serial 203 appeared in 1913. It was powered by a Gnôme rotary engine of 80 hp and the two seats were in tandem enclosed in a single cockpit, shown here with the designer Geoffrey de Havilland sitting in the rear. The machine did not go into production but was taken on the strength of the RFC's 3 Squadron.

PRO ref: AIR 1/2411/303/4/20

The Maurice Farman Shorthorn was a two-seater biplane, fitted with a 70 hp Renault engine, which appeared shortly before the First World War. Intended for reconnaissance, it carried no armament other than the side-arms of its two-man crew. However, some Shorthorns of the RFC's 4 Squadron, which arrived in France in September 1914, were fitted with a Lewis gun in the nacelle, although the weight impaired performance.

MoD ref: H1778

A Maurice Farman Shorthorn used for training in the Middle East.

MoD ref: H1281

Airmen of the RFC with a Leyland transport in 1913.

MoD ref: H1907

This Wight *Navyplane* serial 176, fitted with a Canton Unné pusher engine of 200 hp, first flew on 7 April 1914. Several of these aircraft were ordered by the Admiralty, serial 172 going to the Dardanelles with HMS *Ark Royal*.

PRO ref: AIR 1/479/15/312/239

A Royal Aircraft Factory BE2 of 4 Squadron at the King's Birthday Review on Salisbury Plain in June 1914. The ADC to the King, Lt.-Gen. Sir Horace Smith-Dorrien, was photographed when taking the salute. The horses seem to be unperturbed by the arrival of the aircraft.

MoD ref: H1671

Eight Farmans and four Royal Aircraft Factory BEs of the RFC's 5 Squadron, lined up at Farnborough on 23 April 1914. The squadron moved to France with a variety of types on the outbreak of the First World War and began flying reconnaissance sorties for the British Expeditionary Force over the Western Front.

MoD ref: H2

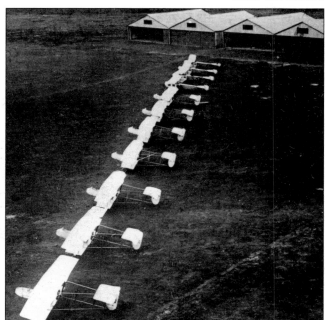

Airmen of the RFC in 1914.

MoD ref: H1906

The 'Concentration Camp' at Netheravon in Wiltshire, where the Military Wing of the RFC gathered for trial mobilization and practice flying over Salisbury Plain, photographed on 29 June 1914.

MoD ref: H5

THE FIRST WORLD WAR

Shortly after the outbreak of war this Royal Aircraft Factory BE2c serial 601 was converted from a BE2a, having been used for many stability experiments at Farnborough during 1913 and 1914 under the direction of the designer Edward T. Busk. On the afternoon of 5 November 1914 Busk took off from Farnborough but the machine caught fire in the air and crashed on Laffan's Plain, resulting in his death.

PRO ref: AIR 1/2411/303/4/20

The RE5 was the first of the Royal Aircraft Factory's Reconnaissance Experimental biplanes to enter production. It appeared over the Western Front in September 1914. The pilot sat in the rear cockpit but neither he nor the observer in the front were armed apart from any personal weapons. It was a very stable aircraft but lacked agility and thus became easy prey for German fighters. The RE5 in this photograph was powered by a Beardmore engine of 120 hp.

PRO ref: AIR 1/2411/303/4/20

The Fokker E-type monoplane, which first appeared over the Western Front in the early summer of 1915, caused such havoc with British and French reconnaissance aircraft that it became known as the 'Fokker scourge'. It was the first German machine to be fitted with an interrupter gear, enabling a Spandau machine-gun to fire through the propeller. Highly manoeuvrable by comparison with British biplanes, the Fokker E-type variants reigned supreme in the skies until better-armed machines began to appear early in 1916. This photograph was taken in 1915.

MoD ref: H1642

Oberleutnant Ernst Freiherr von Althaus, photographed in front of one of the Fokker monoplanes of *Feldfliegerabteilung 23* in 1915. On 21 July 1916 he scored his eighth victory and was awarded the *Pour le Mérite*, Germany's equivalent of the Victoria Cross. He served in various fighter units and commanded both a fighter squadron and a fighter training school. His last victory, the ninth, was scored on 16 July 1917 while he was serving with *Jagdstaffel 10*. He was retired from flying duties at the end of that month as a result of an eye injury, and returned to the Army to command a front-line unit. After the war he became a lawyer. He died in 1946.

MoD ref: H1644

Shortly before the First World War Vickers acquired rights from the German company of Parseval for the British Empire. The non-rigid Parseval HM Airship No. 6, with a length of 312 feet and a volume of 364,000 cubic feet, made her first trials for the Royal Navy at Barrow in 1915. Note the gunner sitting precariously on the top. She served throughout the war and was modified in 1918.

PRO ref: AIR 1/728/176/3/38

Royal Aircraft Factory BE2c serial 1695, showing the Union Jack painted on the rudder. However, before the First World War there was no standard method of distinguishing British military aircraft. When 2, 3, 4 and 5 Squadrons of the RFC flew to France in August 1914, their aircraft carried no national markings other than serial numbers. Later the RFC painted the Union Jack emblem on fuselages and wing undersurfaces, but from a distance the St George's Cross was similar to the German Cross and in any event British troops frequently fired at any aircraft which appeared over their lines. From May 1915 distinctive red, white and blue roundels were painted on the wings, with vertical stripes on the rudder. When aircraft were camouflaged in 1916, the outer blue roundel was outlined by a thin white or yellow circle.

PRO ref: AIR 1/2411/303/4/20

The Royal Aircraft Factory BE2c, known as 'The Quirk', was widely employed by the RFC in front-line service from late 1914 until 1917. Built for stability and ease of flying with a Royal Aircraft Factory 1a engine of 90 hp, it lacked speed, manoeuvrability and ceiling in comparison with the Fokker monoplane which appeared over the Western Front in June 1915. Armed only with a single Lewis gun, fitted either in the pilot's or the observer's cockpit, it earned an unhappy reputation as 'Fokker fodder', even though it remained a very pleasant aircraft to fly when not in combat. This BE2c serial 4162 of the RFC's 16 Squadron was photographed in 1915 at Beaupré Farm in France. The squadron was the first to employ wireless to report reconnaissance, at the Battle of Aubers Ridge in May 1915.

PRO ref: AIR 1/1357/204/19/69

The Albatros C.I was employed mainly on photo-reconnaissance and artillery spotting when it appeared over the Western Front in the spring of 1915, at the time this photograph was taken. It was one of the earliest German machines to be armed, the observer in the rear cockpit being equipped with a machine-gun which had an effective field of fire. German machines were distinguished by the Cross Patée on a white background, known as the Iron Cross, until April 1918.

MoD ref: H1646

Kite balloons began to appear over the Western Front in May 1915, as observation platforms for the British Army. They were modelled on the German *Drachen*, a sausage-shaped design with the forward segment filled with gas and the rear section with air. The mooring cable was attached to the nose of the balloon, which was fitted with rudder, wind sails, and drogue streamers flying from the tail. There is a note by this photograph: 'Parachute shown in position on right of basket'.

PRO ref: AIR 1/728/176/3/38

The Morane-Saulnier Type BB biplane aroused the interest of both the RFC and the RNAS in the summer of 1915. It was a two-seat reconnaissance biplane, fitted with a Le Rhône engine of 110 hp and equipped with two Lewis guns. About eighty were delivered to RFC squadrons in the spring and summer of 1916 but were soon replaced by Nieuport Scouts. This Morane-Saulnier Type BB serial 5167 arrived with 3 Squadron at La Houssoye in France on 19 May 1916, but crashed the following month.

MoD ref: H1783

Women handling one of the SS (Sea Scout) non-rigid airships which were supplied to the RNAS from March 1915 onwards. A gondola with a crew of two was suspended beneath these airships, consisting of the fuselage and engine of a light aircraft and giving an endurance of about sixteen

hours. These airships were mainly used for searching the Dover Strait and the Irish Sea for enemy submarines.

MoD ref: H2333

The Royal Aircraft Factory FE2b was based on the FE2 which first flew in August 1913, but it did not come into service until December 1915. It was armed with up to four machine-guns. One was operated by the pilot for forward fire, with another on a mounting above the centre section for rear defence. The observer in the front cockpit could also be equipped with two guns, one on a bracket firing forward and another on a mounting for firing back over the top plane. The machine was thus provided with an effective defence against the Fokker monoplanes which were causing such havoc with British aircraft. When outclassed by newer German fighters late in 1916, some FE2bs were employed in the night bomber role.

MoD ref: H425

A Royal Aircraft Factory FE2b in flight.

MoD ref: H424

The Short Seaplane, Admiralty Type 184, was a two-seat torpedo bomber produced in 1915 after a torpedo had been dropped successfully from a British aircraft on 28 July 1914. Powered by a Sunbeam Mohawk engine of 225 hp, it was sometimes known as the Short Seaplane 225, even when more powerful engines were fitted. It could carry a 14 inch torpedo or a bomb load up to about 550 lb, and the wings folded back for stowage on aircraft carriers. On 12 August 1915 Flight Commander C.H.K. Edmonds dropped a torpedo from one of these aircraft and sank a Turkish merchant vessel, the first sinking of any ship by aerial torpedo. This type of seaplane continued in service until the end of the war.

PRO ref: AIR 1/7/6/98/7

Cape Helles on the tip of the Gallipoli Peninsula overlooking the strait of the Dardanelles in north-west Turkey, where the British 29th Division landed on 25 April 1915 while the Anzac Corps landed further north. The purpose of the operation was to knock Turkey out of the war and bring relief to the Russians, who were being hard-pressed by German forces on the Eastern Front. The British ships were run aground and enormous casualties were caused by Turkish riflemen as the British troops came out of the sallyports. Nevertheless, a foothold ashore was achieved.

PRO ref: WO 317/1

A searchlight set up on the coast at Soghan Dere in the Gallipoli Peninsula.

PRO ref: WO 317/1

An aerial bomb crater (left) in Gallipoli being examined by British soldiers and Turkish civilians. The Allied forces began to evacuate their positions in December 1915 and on 9 January 1916 the last troops were taken off by the Royal Navy. The enterprise had come near to success but was counted a costly failure.

PRO ref: WO 317/1

On the night of 6/7 June 1915 an incendiary bomb dropped by a Zeppelin fell on a grocery store at 30 Bright Street, Hull. It destroyed the premises although no one was injured. These air attacks resulted in few casualties but caused some panic among British civilians, who had assumed that wars were always fought abroad and that only the military could suffer.

PRO ref: AIR 1/569/16/15/142

This damage at 154 Walker Street, Hull, was caused by an incendiary bomb dropped by a Zeppelin during a raid on the night of 6/7 June 1915. The bomb fell on a partition wall and then through the ceiling on to the landing, setting fire to wallpaper. Godfrey Scott and his wife, seen here, managed to extinguish the fire and later reported that the Zeppelin seemed to be extremely low at the time.

PRO ref: AIR 1/569/16/15/142

The interior of a garage at 109½ Constable Street in Hull after a Zeppelin attack on the night of 6/7 June 1915, showing two Morgan three-wheeler motor cars burnt out by an incendiary bomb.

PRO ref: AIR 1/569/16/15/142

This 110 lb high explosive bomb was dropped at Wolferton in Norfolk during August 1916, but it failed to explode and the detonator was detached. It was photographed next to an incendiary bomb.

PRO ref: AIR 1/566/16/15/112

The ruins after a great fire at Davis's drapery store and the Fleece Inn in Hull after a Zeppelin attack on the night of 6/7 June 1915. The heat of the fire melted the lead of some of the stained glass windows of the church on the right, but a north-west wind kept the fire away from it as well as from the premises on the left. It was thought at first that there were no casualties but the body of an unidentified woman was found ten days later under the debris.

PRO ref: AIR 1/569/16/15/142

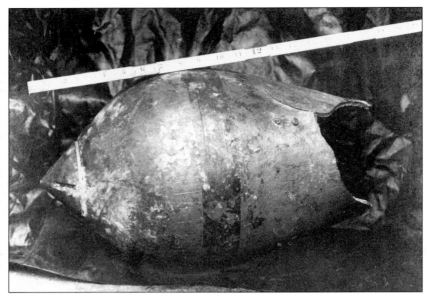

This high explosive bomb was dropped in the Joint Stock Old Quarry, near Durham, on 8 August 1916. The circumference was 35¼ inches and the estimated height of the complete bomb case was 31 inches. It was filled with crude TNT and the weight when complete was estimated as 200 lb.

PRO ref: AIR 1/566/16/15/122

On 2 May 1916 eight German Naval Zeppelins and one Army Zeppelin were ordered to bomb Royal Navy bases in Scotland and industrial targets in northern England. One of these, *L20* – commanded by *Kapitänleutnant* Franz Stabbart – dropped some bombs near Craig Castle and then ran out of fuel on the return journey. The Zeppelin came down in a fjord near Stavanger in Norway, where she broke in two.

PRO ref: AIR 1/7/6/98

On 23 September 1916 eleven German Naval Zeppelins set off to bomb targets in England. One of these, *L33* – commanded by *Kapitänleutnant* Böcker – dropped some bombs over north-east London but was hit by anti-aircraft fire as well as by machine-gun fire from a BE2c of 39 Squadron flown by 2nd Lt. Alfred de B. Brandon from Sutton's Farm in Essex. All the crewmen were unhurt. Böcker set his Zeppelin on fire and then marched his men along a road where they surrendered to Special Constable Edgar Nicholas, who was cycling towards the blaze. The remains of the Zeppelin became an object of great interest to the military and the general public.

PRO ref: AIR 1/7/6/98

The Naval Zeppelin *L64*, 536 feet long and 61 feet wide after rebuilding, photographed in 1918. She first flew on 11 March 1918 and her twenty-six flights included thirteen reconnaissance missions, one raid on Britain and an air battle with six RAF fighters. She survived the war and even the occasion when the German flight crews, taking their cue from the post-war scuttling of the German Fleet at Scapa Flow, entered the Zeppelin sheds and wrecked five ships at Nordholz and two more at Wittmundhaven. *L64* was untouched at Alhorn and taken to Britain but was destroyed by storms on 21 July 1920.

PRO ref: ADM 137/4125

Crew members of a Zeppelin, probably photographed in 1918.

PRO ref: ADM 137/4125

The Nieuport 12 (or Scout) was a two-seat reconnaissance aircraft armed with a Vickers gun firing forward and another machine-gun in the observer's position. Deliveries to RFC and RNAS squadrons in France began in early 1916 and the machine enjoyed some success until early the following year when it became outclassed by German fighters. Some Nieuport Scouts were then transferred to home defence or used for training.

MoD ref: H1784

The Royal Aircraft Factory RE7 was a modified RE5 designed primarily to carry the new 336 lb bomb which was developed shortly after the outbreak of war. First models were powered by Beardmore engines of 120 hp or 160 hp, but some later models were fitted with Royal Aircraft Factory 4a engines of 150 hp. The RE7 entered service in January 1916 as the first of the RFC's 'heavy bombers'. Attempts were made to fit a Lewis gun in the front cockpit and some RE7s were modified to include a third cockpit with a Lewis gun on a Scarff ring. This RE7 serial 2348 was fitted with a Royal Aircraft Factory 4a engine but later converted to a three-seater with a Beardmore engine.

PRO ref: AIR 1/2411/303/4/20

The Martinsyde Elephant, designed as a single-seat escort for long range bombers, earned its name from its unusually large size. It came into service in early 1916 but proved too heavy and unresponsive for aerial fighting and was switched to the role of bombing and ground attack, in which it proved very successful. Serial 7474 in this photograph was armed with two 230 lb bombs, bound with rope to prevent deep penetration and thus achieve greater lateral blast. It was on the strength of 14 Squadron based in the Middle East.

MoD ref: H1232

The Sopwith triplane was built on the assumption that the decreased wing span and increased area would improve climbing and manoeuvring ability. It proved an outstanding success when it was tested by the RNAS in France in May 1916. Deliveries to the RNAS and the RFC began the following November, and the new machine was eagerly accepted, although it was given the unflattering nickname 'Tripehound'. Armed with a centrally mounted Vickers gun synchronized to fire through the propeller, it continued in service throughout the remainder of the war. It preceded the Fokker Dr1 triplane which appeared in August 1917.

MoD ref: H1950

This 'Periscopic Bomb Sight' was developed by the Royal Aircraft Factory and tested on single-seater Martinsyde Elephants during the summer of 1916. To operate the instrument on bombing attacks, the pilot had first to estimate the wind direction, usually by observing any drift when objects passed down the sighting wire at the eye cap marked 'A'. Then, by means of spotting a convenient ground position on his map, he had to approach the target from either up-wind or down-wind. Lateral level of the bomb sight was adjusted before take-off by the level at 'G'. The fore and aft level was adjusted at 'E' by turning the knurled screw head at 'F' until the bubble was central. The pilot was expected to keep his left eye on the bubble and his right eye on the eye cap. Height of the aircraft was set by an adjustment on the drum 'C'. Ground speed was set on the same drum by starting a stopwatch at the time a conspicuous object passed the crosswire at the eye cap, then turning the drum to the right until it reached the stop (vertical) position, and stopping the watch at the time it passed the crosswire again. This gave the graduation in seconds to be set on the drum's time scale, which in turn gave the correct bombing angle. Then the pilot had to continue and release the bomb or bombs when the target appeared on the crosswire. The instructions assured the pilot that all this was possible with a little practice, although no mention was made of any enemy action which might divert his attention.

PRO ref: AIR 1/756/204/4/91

The Halberstadt CL.II Scout, a two-seater with a communal cockpit, appeared in mid-1916. Designed for close support escort, it was armed with one or two Spandau machine-guns firing through the propeller and a Parabellum on a ring mounting firing to the rear. Usually powered by a Mercedes engine of 170 hp, it was also used for light bombing and ground attack, and indeed proved very effective against British troops in this role. This Halberstadt CL.II was forced down behind British lines by the Commanding Officer of 15 Squadron, Major D.F. Stevenson, in 1918, at a time when his squadron was equipped with RE8s and most CL.IIs had been withdrawn from the Western Front. On 15 April 1918 Germany introduced the Balkan Cross in black edged with white as its national insignia.

MoD ref: H1126

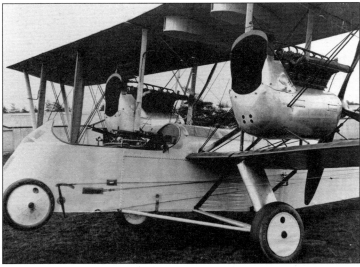

Only two Royal Aircraft Factory FE4s were produced, in an attempt to provide a multi-purpose bomber and fighter. These were serials 7993 and 7994 which appeared in 1916. The pilot sat in the front seat and behind him was a gunner, with yet another gunner aft of the wings. The original intention was to arm a fighter version with the 1½-pounder Coventry Aircraft Works gun, but serial 7994 in this photograph was fitted with two Lewis guns. The aircraft proved so slow and unwieldy that proposals for production were abandoned. All the available engines, Rolls-Royce 190 hp, were allocated to the new Bristol Fighter.

PRO ref: AIR 1/2411/303/4/20

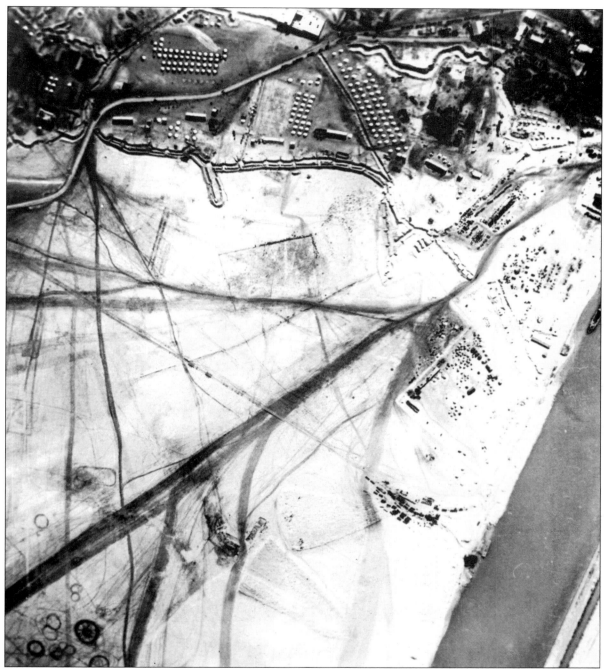

This vertical photograph of Kantara (or Qantara) in Egypt was taken from 6,000 feet on 30 January 1916 by a Royal Aircraft Factory BE2c of 14 Squadron. A flight of this squadron was based in the town, which is about 27 miles south of Port Said and is alongside the Suez Canal (bottom right).

PRO ref: AIR 1/449/15/307/1

The Royal Aircraft Factory FE8 was the last of the single-seat fighters with a pusher engine to enter service with the RFC, in July 1916. Although fitted with only a single Lewis gun on a pivot mounting in front of the cockpit, it achieved some success on the Western Front until replaced by tractor fighters. Only three squadrons were equipped with FE8s and it was withdrawn from front-line service in July 1917. It was regarded as an easy aircraft to fly, but this reputation was not achieved until a test pilot put one into a spin and recovered safely. The caption on this photograph of the second prototype, serial 7456, purports to show this event, but the propeller is not turning and there is no pilot in the cockpit. It is thus a fake, compiled from a photograph taken on the ground superimposed on a cloud scene.

PRO ref: AIR 1/2411/303/4/20

The prototype of the Royal Aircraft Factory FE8 was unarmed when it first flew in October 1915, but a stripped down Lewis gun on a de Havilland pivot mounting was installed on a later model, as shown in this photograph dated January 1916.

PRO ref: AIR 1/942/204/5/972

The Royal Aircraft Factory FE2d was an improvement on earlier models of the design, with an increase of wingspan to 49 feet and the installation of a Rolls-Royce Eagle engine of 250 hp, raising the airspeed to 95 mph and the ceiling to about 17,500 feet. The machine was armed with four Lewis guns, two of which were operated by the observer in the front seat, and it gave a good account of itself when it appeared over the Western Front in the summer of 1916.

PRO ref: AIR 1/2411/303/4/20

This prototype of the Bristol Monoplane Scout was photographed on 8 August 1916. It had been tested at the Central Flying School during the previous month, where it was found to have an excellent performance, attaining 128 mph at 5,400 feet, although the downward view from the cockpit was considered poor. It was anticipated that this machine, fitted with a Vickers gun firing through the propeller, would achieve mastery of the air over the Germans. However, the RFC had developed such an antipathy towards monoplanes, following numerous accidents before the war, that it was not until 3 August 1917 that a contract was placed for 125 Monoplane Scouts. These were not produced soon enough to serve on the Western Front, but a few were sent to Macedonia and the Middle East, although they arrived too late to make much difference in these theatres of war.

PRO ref: AIR 1/2535

HM Airship No. 9 was the first of Britain's non-rigid airships to fly, on 27 November 1916. After modification, she was accepted by the Royal Navy on 4 April 1917. Her length was 526 feet and her volume 889,300 cubic feet. She was not a success, spending most of her time in mooring and handling experiments, and was dismantled in June 1918.

PRO ref: AIR 1/728/176/3/38

In 1916 the Royal Aircraft Factory fitted some BE2cs with armour weighing 445 lb. These were employed on ground attack against German troops on the Western Front, with some success.

PRO ref: AIR 1/2411/303/4/20

The Royal Aircraft Factory RE8 was the most widely used British two-seater on the Western Front, being employed on reconnaissance, ground attack and night bombing. Powered by a Royal Aircraft Factory 4a engine of 150 hp, it entered service in November 1916, and became known in Cockney rhyming slang as the 'Harry Tate' after a music-hall comedian. It was armed with a Vickers gun firing through the propeller and a Lewis gun on a Scarff ring in the rear cockpit. Although outclassed by German fighters which caused heavy losses, it continued in front-line service until the end of the war.

PRO ref: AIR 1/2411/303/4/20

Royal Aircraft Factory RE8 serial C2670. This aircraft was one of a batch subcontracted to the Daimler Co. Ltd of Coventry.

PRO ref: AIR 1/7/6/98/9

The Vickers FB26, later named the Vampire, was powered by a Hispano Suiza pusher engine of 200 hp. The prototype crashed into the ground on 25 August 1917, killing the pilot, and the cause of the accident was never established. The Vampire was fitted with two Lewis guns in the nose, later increased to three. It was intended for home defence, but only three of the six ordered were built, of which serial B1484 in this photograph was the first.

MoD ref: B1951

The Bristol Fighter, a two-seater, first went into action over the Western Front in April 1917 and eventually proved remarkably successful. Many were built after the war for both home and overseas squadrons. This Bristol Fighter F2B Mark II serial J6774 was a post-war aircraft which served with 5 Squadron when based at Quetta in India. It continued until 1931 but others remained in service until 1932.

MoD ref: H1069

Royal Aircraft Factory FE2b of 100 Squadron, carrying one 230 lb bomb, two 20 lb bombs and two flares for night operations. The squadron was formed with these aircraft in the night bomber role on 11 February 1917 and moved to France about six weeks later. In August 1918 it became part of the RAF's Independent Force and was equipped with Handley Page O/400s for strategic bombing at night. This aircraft, serial A5478, was one of the first manufactured by Boulton & Paul Ltd, then at Norwich.

MoD ref: H1766

This Fairey Hamble Baby, a small single-seat aircraft employed by the RNAS on coastal and anti-submarine patrols, crashed into a wireless mast at Horsey Island, Portsmouth, and remained stuck like a fly on a spider's web. The pilot, Flight Commander E.A. de Ville, survived and managed to descend to the ground.

MoD ref: H482

The Lewis gun on a Scarff ring in the observer's position gave the Bristol Fighter a sting in the tail which surprised many enemy pilots. Forward armament consisted of a Vickers gun firing through the propeller. The highly manoeuvrable, rugged and popular Bristol Fighter was known as the 'Biff' or the 'Brisfit'.

MoD ref: H66

HRH The Prince of Wales photographed in the observer's cockpit of a Bristol Fighter of 139 Squadron in northern Italy in 1918. The pilot was believed to have been Captain Dalrymple. The squadron was formed in Italy on 3 July 1918 with Bristol Fighters and remained operational on the Piave front until the end of the war.

MoD ref: H1608

The Royal Aircraft Factory SE5a achieved the distinction of being one of the most famous fighters of the First World War, sharing honours with the Sopwith Camel. In its earlier form of the SE5, with a less powerful engine, it entered RFC service in March 1917. The SE5a followed about three months later and soon established a high reputation for its flying qualities and ruggedness. It was normally armed with a Vickers gun firing through the propeller and a Lewis gun on the centre section operated by a Bowden cable, but the SE5a serial D3943 in this photograph was fitted with a Hythe gun camera for practice air-to-air combat.

MoD ref: H433

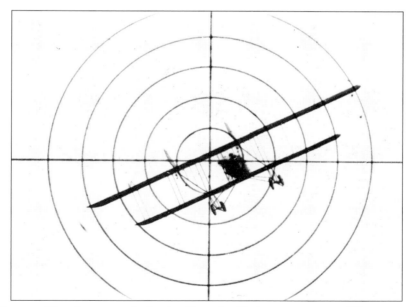

A Maurice Farman Shorthorn caught in the film of a Hythe gun camera. The concentric rings of the gun sight enabled the attacking pilot to estimate the distance of the 'enemy' aircraft as well as its movement relative to his own. He then pressed the trigger and obtained what was usually a deflection shot, in which bullets would have scored hits.

MoD ref: H1851

These films from a Hythe gun camera were taken on 20 September 1918 during mock combat between an SE5a flown by Lt. T.S. Horry of 92 Squadron and another flown by Capt. J.M. Robb. The squadron was based in France and engaged on fighter and ground attack duties over the Western Front, but such practice was valuable for improving flying skills.

MoD ref: H1171

This Gotha G.IV biplane was brought down on 23 April 1917 near Vron in France by a fighter of the RNAS. It was then set on fire by its crew of three. The pilot had not intended to cross the lines but mistook Abbeville in the British sector for Valenciennes, which was occupied by the Germans. The wreckage of this aircraft became the subject of a detailed report. Soon afterwards, Gotha long-range bombers caused considerable dismay when they began daylight raids over southern England, replacing the night attacks by Zeppelins. The first daylight raid on London took place on 13 June 1917 and caused over six hundred casualties.

PRO ref: AIR 1/5/4/26/29

This photograph of a Spad VII serial A6706 of the RFC's 19 Squadron, shot down behind enemy lines, was taken from a German prisoner-of-war, Musketeer M.W. Kirsche. The squadron was equipped with these machines from December 1916 to June 1917 when based on various airfields in France. The Spad (*Societé Pour l'Aviation et ses Derivées)* VII was a fast fighter with an excellent climbing ability which was supplied to French, British and Belgian squadrons at a time when the RFC was mainly reliant on ageing machines with pusher engines.

MoD ref: H1179

A message from the German Air Force dropped on a British airfield in France in early February 1917. It was translated by the British as:

To the Royal Flying Corps.

List of British airmen recently shot down in the German lines (in reply to enquiry dropped down about the location of Lieutenants Alder and White, 20th Squadron).

23.1.17	Lieut. Lyle Subaltern Harrison }	45th Squadron. Both dead.
	Lieut. Cody	41st do dead.
24.1.17	Lieut. Buck Pilot (could not be identified) }	53rd Squadron. Both dead.
25.1.17	Lieut. Alder Lieut. White }	20th Squadron. Both slightly wounded, in captivity.
26.1.17	Pilot Flemig Machine gunner Webb }	Both dead.
1.2.17	Captain Carbert Lieut. Spicer }	20th Squadron. Both dead. (Machine No. A'28)

Further on 1.2.17 a machine of the 20th Squadron, the crew taken prisoners.

A Division of German Airmen

At the time these aircraft were shot down, 45 Squadron was equipped with Sopwith 1½-Strutters and based at St Marie Cappel, 41 Squadron with Royal Aircraft Factory FE8s at Abeele, 53 Squadron with Royal Aircraft Factory BE2cs at Bailleul, and 20 Squadron with Royal Aircraft Factory FE8s at Boisdinghem.

PRO ref: AIR 1/435/15/273/11

```
Copy of message dropped from a  German Aeroplane - extracted
from 87/Accidents/70. (24.4.17)
                                -------------

Royal Flying Corps.

        British Aviator was shot down to-day between 12 and
1 o'clock.  Shot in the stomach.    More particulars will
follow.    Has just died.


                                       12.3.17.
                                    German  Flying Corps.
        B.A. 157.
                        --------------------------------

        N.B. This message refers to 2/Lieut. D.H.Glasson, R.F.C. No. 47
        Squadron and has been accepted for official purposes.    List No.
        B.6557. (10th. My, 1917).
```

A copy of a message from the German Air Force dropped on a British airfield in France on 12 March 1917.

PRO ref: AIR 1/435/15/273/11

The A-type camera was manufactured by the Thornton-Pickard Company from a design by Lts. J.T.C. Moore-Brabazon and C.D.M. Campbell in early 1915, from their experiences of flying over the Western Front. It took a series of plates measuring 5 inches by 4 inches and was intended to be mounted vertically on the side of an aircraft or hand-held by straps. When 30 Squadron RFC was based in Iraq during February 1917, Corporal Parton suggested that a bracket be made which enabled an A-type to point downwards at an angle of 25 degrees from the vertical.

PRO ref: AIR 1/901/204/5/759

In June 1917 the A-type camera was fitted to the side of a BE2c of 30 Squadron based in Baghdad. On 8 June 1917 the machine was flown at various altitudes and it was considered that 6,000 feet would be the best for trench warfare, giving a coverage of about 4 miles over the ground. This example showed the town of Moazzam looking south-east, with the photograph gridded for purposes of photo-interpretation.

PRO ref: AIR 1/901/204/5/759

Pilots and observers studying maps beside an Armstrong Whitworth FK8 in April 1918. The FK8, a scaled-up version of the earlier FK3, was delivered to RFC squadrons towards the end of 1916 and served for the remainder of the war. Known as the 'Big Ack', it was a two-seater employed on reconnaissance, day and night bombing, and ground attack. It was highly regarded by the crews, being robustly built and well defended with a Vickers gun firing through the propeller and a Lewis gun on a Scarff ring for the observer.

MoD ref: H2338

The Sopwith F1 Camel first entered service on the Western Front in June 1917. Fitted with a Le Rhône engine and two Vickers guns firing through the propeller, it proved fast and highly manoeuvrable, although its eccentricities made it so difficult to fly that many novice pilots died in the attempt. It achieved the distinction of destroying more enemy aircraft than any other type and is regarded by many as the most famous fighter of the First World War.

MoD ref: H305

A Sopwith 2F1 Camel of the RNAS, with one Vickers gun mounted to port above the engine and firing through the propeller, and a free-handling Lewis gun mounted on the centre section of the top plane. Such Camels could be flown from aircraft carriers or catapulted from other vessels, and were employed against German seaplanes and Zeppelins. This photograph was probably taken in 1918.

PRO ref: AIR 1/728/176/3/38

In 1918 attempts were made to protect airships by carrying fighter aircraft. This Sopwith 2F1 Camel serial N6622 was suspended below **HM Airship** *R23* when flying from Pulham. The first live release was made by a pilot of 212 Squadron, but the end of the war arrived before the method could be used in operational flying.

PRO ref: AIR 1/306/15/226/169

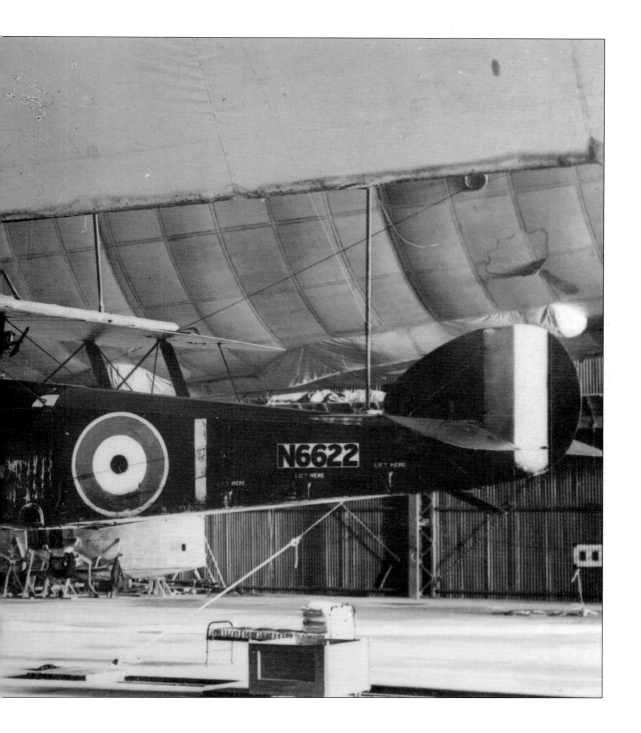

The strong system of defences known as the *Siegfried-Stellung* by the Germans was named the 'Hindenburg Line' by the British after Field Marshal Paul von Hindenburg, who was appointed as the German Chief of General Staff on 29 August 1916. It stretched behind the German front lines from Arras through Saint-Quentin to Laffaux, 6 miles north-east of Soissons, and was completed in early 1917. Many RFC reconnaissance aircraft were lost in attempting to photograph its entire length, of which this stretch south-west of Bullecourt taken on 6 April 1917 is an example. The Germans withdrew to this line in April 1917 to escape artillery pounding and probing attacks by the British. They destroyed all buildings and trees in their retreat, and shortened their front line by 26 miles.

PRO ref: AIR 34/735

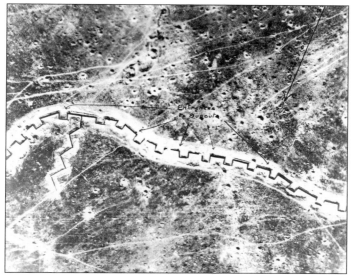

A vertical photograph of German trenches on the Western Front, with surrounding shell holes. The photo-interpreters could also pick out covered entrances to dugouts. The direction of the light was from the top part of the photograph, casting shadows towards the viewer and providing the best aspect for looking at any vertical photograph.

PRO ref: AIR 34/735

The Messines Ridge, near Ypres in the West Flanders district of Belgium, photographed on 29 April 1917 by a BE2c of the RFC's 6 Squadron based at Abeele. The photograph showed British and German trenches, with No Man's Land between them, and the countryside pockmarked with shell holes.

PRO ref: WO 158/306

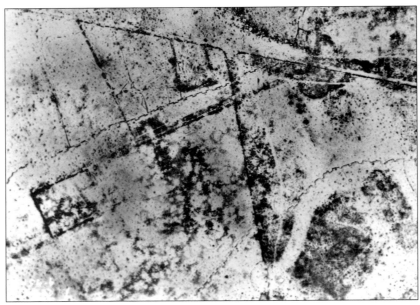

The same area of Messines Ridge photographed on 11 June 1917 by a BE2c of the RFC's 6 Squadron, by which time the battleground resembled a lunar landscape. The battle continued until 10 November but no breakthrough was achieved, although the British advanced a few miles. Each side suffered about 240,000 casualties between 31 July and 10 November, including about 37,000 German prisoners.

PRO ref: WO 158/306

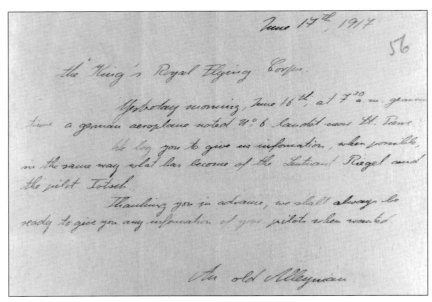

A message from the German Air Force dropped on a British airfield in France on 17 June 1917. The signature 'An old Alleyman' indicates that the Germans were aware of the term used by British soldiers, which was a corruption of the French word 'Allemand'.

PRO ref: AIR 1/435/15/273/11

The seaplane station at Fishguard in Pembrokeshire, with a Short 184 seaplane on the hardstanding outside the hangar, together with what appears to be a Sopwith Baby. The photograph was taken on 31 July 1917.

PRO ref: AIR 59/8

A DH4 used for parachuting experiments at RAF Northolt in Middlesex during 1919.

MoD ref: H1947

The Airco DH4 was the first British aircraft designed for day bombing. It entered service with the RFC on the Western Front during March 1917, and other deliveries were made to the RNAS. The two-seat DH4 had the ability to fly above enemy fighters and was also employed on photo-reconnaissance duties. Some served in the Middle East and later in Russia. Many were produced in the United States under licence. This DH4 serial N5997 was made by the subcontractors Westland

Aircraft Works at Yeovil and was on the strength of 202 Squadron, which was equipped with these machines from April 1918 to March 1919 when serving on the Western Front and later in Germany.

MoD ref: H1536

Capt. James T.B. McCudden with his dog 'Bruiser'. He joined the RFC as a mechanic from the Royal Engineers in May 1913 and eventually qualified as a pilot. He was awarded the Croix de Guerre in January 1916 and the Military Medal in September of that year. His commission came through in January 1917. He was awarded the Military Cross the following month, with a Bar in October. The Distinguished Service Order followed in December of that year, with a Bar in January 1918. He was gazetted with the Victoria Cross in April 1918, by which time he had been credited with fifty-four enemy aircraft, forty-two of which had been definitely destroyed. Promoted to Temporary Major in July 1918, he was appointed to command 60 Squadron (equipped with SE5as) but was killed in an air accident at Marquise on the 9th of that month.

MoD ref: H1175

This photograph of the RFC's 56 Squadron orchestra was taken in 1917. The squadron was based at London Colney in Hertfordshire at the beginning of the year but moved to France on 7 April, when it was equipped with Royal Aircraft Factory SE5 single-seater fighters.

MoD ref: H2028

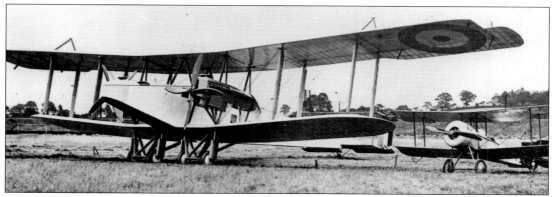

Handley Page O/100 of the RNAS photographed in 1918 with Bristol Scout C serial 3026. The O/100 first appeared in December 1915 in response to a demand from the Admiralty requiring a 'bloody paralyser of a bomber' capable of bombing Germany. Most of the forty-six built were powered by two Rolls-Royce Eagle II engines of 250 hp and they could carry up to 2,000 lb of bombs. The first version of the Scout, which was sometimes called the Bullet, appeared shortly before the First World War. Fitted with either a Le Rhône or a Gnôme engine of 80 hp, the first machines were unarmed but some were later fitted with a machine-gun. The O/100 was followed in service by the more numerous O/400 and by 1918 the Scout had been withdrawn from front-line service.

PRO ref: AIR 1/7/6/98/2

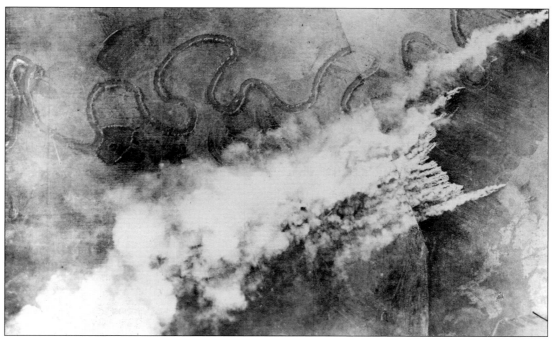

A German smoke-screen alongside the meandering River Oise, photographed by the French Air Force over their sector of the Western Front. Two photographs taken in sequence were joined to provide this result, called a mosaic.

PRO ref: AIR 10/1120

An example of a German aerodrome behind the lines, showing a landing 'T' and a smoke signal giving the direction of the wind for landing and take-off.

PRO ref: AIR 34/735

A German battery moving off on to a road, photographed in the Arras sector of the Western Front.

PRO ref: AIR 10/1120

The same German battery, with personnel scattering across open country after being attacked by machine-gun fire from the aircraft.

PRO ref: AIR 10/1120

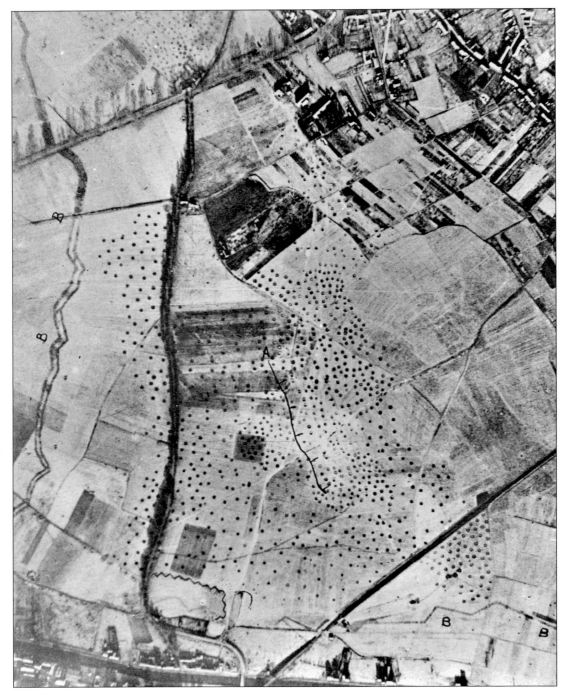

Pairs of shell holes, marked A in this photograph, were protected by the Germans using barbed wire. Photo-interpreters were able to pick out much activity around them. The area was between Carvin and Pont de Courrières, north-east of Arras.

PRO ref: AIR 10/1120

This aerodrome at Bailleul in France, midway between Dunkirk and Lille, was the home of several RFC squadrons during the First World War. No. 1 Squadron was based there from March 1915 to March 1918.

PRO ref: AIR 1/1078/204/5/1679

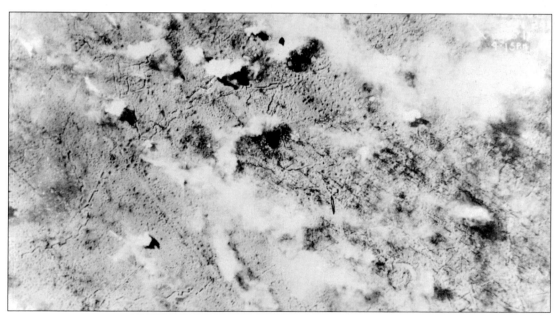

Part of a British barrage against German positions on the Messines Ridge, photographed on 6 June 1917 by a BE2c of the RFC's 6 Squadron, after 2,226 guns of all calibres had opened up several days earlier on a front of 8½ miles. The day after this photograph was taken, nineteen mines were exploded under the German positions. Commonwealth divisions then went over the top to attack.

PRO ref: WO 158/306

When the Hannoveraner CL.III appeared over the Western Front in late 1917 the Allies believed from its compact outline that it was a single-seat fighter. It was later realized that it was a two-seater employed on reconnaissance and ground attack, powered by an Opel-Argun engine of 180 hp. The machine was particularly active in artillery spotting during the German offensive in the spring of 1918. Although armed with a Spandau machine-gun firing through the propeller and a Parabellum on a ring for the observer, Allied fighters were able to attack it from behind and below. This captured Hannoveraner CL.III number C13103 was painted with RAF insignia and taken on charge by 87 Squadron, which was based at Boussières in France at the time of the Armistice.

PRO ref: AIR 1/1227/204/5/2634/87

This photograph of Trier (Trèves) in Germany was taken after a bombing attack during the night of 18/19 February 1918 by eight FE2bs of 100 Squadron based at Ochey near Nancy, where it was part of the RFC's 41st Wing which was formed in October 1917 to attack German industry within its reach. One FE2b failed to return. The crews of the others dropped ten bombs and reported direct hits on the railway station as well as a big fire.

PRO ref: AIR 1/1998/204/273/264

```
                              April 20th, 1918.

                              6.43 p.m.

                              north-east of Villers-
                                  Bretonneux.

Sopwith Camel.                Englishman.

                              Fok. Dr. I 425/17, red
                                  painting.

                              Burned.

            - - - - - - - - - - - - - - - -

     Three minutes after I had brought down the first machine
I attacked a second Camel of the same enemy squad.   The
adversary dived, caught his machine and repeated this manoeuvre
several times.   I approached him as near as possible when
fighting and fired 50 bullets until the machine began to burn.
The body of the machine was burned in the air, the remnants
dashed to the ground north-east of Villers-Bretonneux.


                         (Signed)  FRHR.  V. RICHTHOFEN.
                              Captain and Squadron Commander.


Pursuit Squadron 1.
Nr. 446 I.


                              O.U.  April 20th, 1918.



     To Commanding Officer of Air Forces 2.

Requesting to effect acknowledgement of 80th victory from
            highest command.



                         (Signed)  FRHR.  V.  RICHTHOFEN.
                              Captain and Squadron Commander.
```

British translation of the report of the eightieth and final victory of Baron Manfred von Richtofen, Commander of the 11th Squadron (Richtofen's Flying Circus), dated 20 April 1918.

PRO ref: AIR 1/2397/262/1

The Fokker D.VII was considered the finest single-seat fighter produced by Germany in the war, partly since it had the ability to maintain good performance at high altitudes. It first appeared in the summer of 1918 and scored many victories over the Western Front. Powered by a Mercedes engine of 160 hp and armed with twin Spandau machine-guns firing through the propeller, it had a maximum speed of 120 mph at sea level and a service ceiling of about 18,000 feet. This Fokker D.VII was photographed at RAF Biggin Hill in Kent in May 1919.

MoD ref: H1128

The inland docks at Bruges in Belgium, connected by canals to Ostend and Zeebrugge, were targets for three squadrons of RAF bombers allocated to Vice-Admiral Sir Roger Keyes of the Dover Patrol in the spring of 1918. They were mainly attacked by 214 Squadron, which was formed on 1 April 1918 from two former RNAS squadrons and based at Coudekerque in France. The squadron was first equipped with Handley Page O/100s and then with O/400s from June. This U-boat was photographed by the Germans after being damaged by an RAF bomb in a floating dock at Bruges.

PRO ref: AIR 1/2121/207/56/2

This German photograph of a torpedo boat, the size of a small destroyer, was taken looking north-east in the East Basin at Bruges, after bombing by the RAF in 1918.

PRO ref: AIR 1/2121/207/56/2

The remains of a German destroyer alongside a merchant ship in the docks at Bruges. It had been damaged by an RAF bomb and was later demolished by the Germans during their evacuation of the port.

PRO ref: AIR 1/2121/207/56/2

Zeebrugge mole and seaplane station in Belgium, which was the scene of the storming and blocking operation by seamen and marines of the Royal Navy on the night of 22/23 April 1918, under Vice-Admiral Sir Roger Keyes. This was preceded by a bombing attack by the RAF. The purpose was to close the port and prevent German U-boats and destroyers from operating in the Strait of Dover. The landing party came under tremendous fire but two blockships were sunk and partially closed the port. Eight Victoria Crosses were awarded, some chosen by ballot. A similar operation at Ostend on the same night failed, since two blockships were sunk by enemy fire before reaching their objective.

PRO ref: ADM 137/4123

Anti-aircraft gun defences at Zeebrugge.

PRO ref: ADM 137/4123

Machine-gun defences at Zeebrugge.

PRO ref: ADM 137/4123

Field Marshal Paul von Hindenburg (in Army uniform), who was appointed as the German Chief of General Staff on 29 August 1916, photographed in company with Admiral von Schroeder and officers of the Marine Korps when visiting Zeebrugge mole and seaplane station. The photograph was not dated.

PRO ref: ADM 137/4123

Destruction in the dry dock shelter for U-boats at Ostend, photographed by the Germans after bombardment from the sea by the Royal Navy.

PRO ref: AIR 1/2121/207/56/2

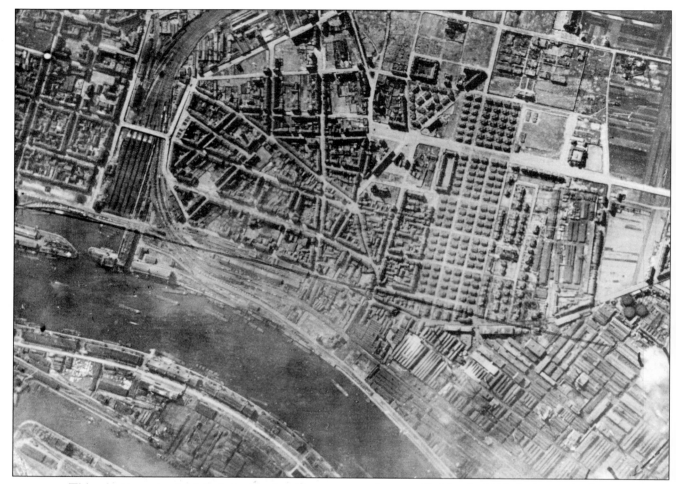

This photograph of Mannheim/Ludwigshaven was taken on 18 March 1918 during a daylight attack by nine DH4s of 55 Squadron based at Tantonville in France, where it formed part of the RFC's 41st Wing. The DH4s were attacked by enemy fighters over the target, but two of these were reported to have been driven off out of control. No DH4s were lost. Direct hits were reported on a chemical works, with fires started. The Germans recorded that four people were killed and ten injured.

PRO ref: AIR 1/2419/305/9

The LVG (*Luft-Verkehrs Gesellschaft*) C.VI two-seater appeared over the Western Front in 1918, superseding earlier Marks of the aircraft by improving the design and performance. It was a multi-purpose aircraft, used for artillery spotting, photo-reconnaissance and bombing. Armed with a forward-firing Spandau and a rear-mounted Parabellum, it was also capable of effective defence against Allied fighters.

PRO ref: AIR 10/475

This poster was displayed by the mayor of the German town of Düren, near Cologne, after an attack by the RAF on 1 August 1918. It read:

Air Raid Warning!
Two minute warbling note of siren and the firing of pyrotechnics means:
Air Raid Warning!
All trams are to stop and everyone is to take cover
A steady siren note of one minute means:
All Clear
The 'All Clear' signal will be sounded at 6 o'clock every evening for a quarter of a minute.

In fact, Düren was not attacked again.
PRO ref: AIR 1/1998/204/273/264

A German air raid siren was installed when the RFC and RNAS began bombing industrial centres, railways and ports in Germany in retaliation for air attacks against Britain.

PRO ref: AIR 1/1998/204/27/267

A crater in the ground of the Oppau Chemical Works at Mannheim, made by a 230 lb bomb dropped on the night of 17/18 May 1918 by one of three Handley Page O/400s of 216 Squadron based at Ochey in France. The factory was forced to close down for two days since a bomb fractured a gas main.

PRO ref: AIR 1/1998/204/273/265

This crater was made by a 1,650 lb bomb dropped on the night of 9/10 August 1918 by a Handley Page O/400 of the RAF's Independent Force, which was formed on 6 June 1918. It fell in the grounds of the *Clinique des Petites Soeurs Françaises* in Bruges but apparently caused no damage to this hospital.

PRO ref: AIR 1/2121/207/56/2

This photograph was taken in August 1918 in front of a Handley Page O/400 of 207 Squadron based at Ligescourt in France, where it formed part of the RAF's 54th Wing. It shows the largest bomb in the RAF, a 1,650 lb SN Mark I labelled A LITTLE HELL(P) FROM THE RAF, with the smallest, a 20 lb Cooper, propped up against it.

MoD ref: H2339

An oblique photograph of trenches and a British Army encampment near Sammarrah in Mesopotamia, as the lower and middle reaches of the Rivers Tigris and Euphrates were called in the First World War. It was taken from 1,000 feet on 2 June 1918. British and Indian troops had occupied the area during the previous year.

PRO ref: AIR 10/1001

A line of German rifle pits behind a river at Baisieux in the Valenciennes sector, photographed on 30 October 1918 during the last stages of the war when the Germans were retreating in front of the advancing British, American and French armies.

PRO ref: AIR 10/1120

On the night of 14/15 September 1918 the RAF's Independent Force despatched forty Handley Page O/400s from France to attack railways, mainly at Metz in Germany. The squadrons involved were 97, 100 and 215 at Xaffévillers and 216 at Autreville. Metz-Sablon station was damaged, as shown in this photograph, with four people killed and eleven injured. Nine bombers returned early with engine trouble, one force-landed behind British lines, and three failed to return.

PRO ref: AIR 1/2419/305/9

The Short 320 was the last of the seaplanes employed by the RAF in the First World War. It appeared in August 1918 and was engaged on anti-submarine patrols and naval reconnaissance. This Short 320 was photographed while practising torpedo-dropping. Four RAF squadrons were equipped with these machines, but they were withdrawn from service in October 1919.

MoD ref: H265

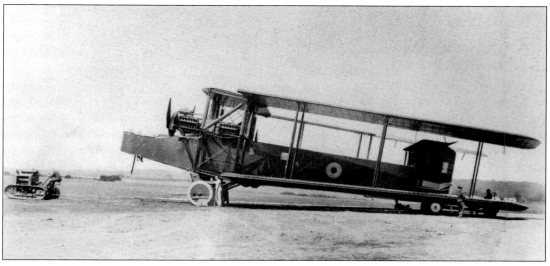

The Handley Page V/1500 was the largest British bomber to enter service in the First World War. Fitted with four Rolls-Royce Eagle VIII engines, it was designed to bring Berlin within reach of the RAF. However, the Armistice was signed when the first aircraft, with 166 Squadron at Bircham Newton in Norfolk, were standing by to take off. Shortly after the Armistice a Handley Page V/1500 made the initial through flight from England to India. Although V/1500s did not remain long in service, they heralded the formation of the RAF's strategic bombing force.

MoD ref: H1561

The pilot's cockpit of a Handley Page V/1500. The machine was armed with single or twin Lewis guns in four positions, was crewed by up to seven men, and could carry a maximum bomb load of 7,500 lb (usually thirty 250 lb bombs).

MoD ref: H1675

The hangars and installations on the German airfield at Boulay in reconquered Lorraine had been almost entirely dismantled by French civilians by the time the British arrived to examine the effects of RAF bombing, which had taken place by day and night. However, the French reported that all had received direct hits and suffered considerably. All the remaining German aircraft, such as this Friedrichshafen G.IIIa bomber, had been riddled by splinters and rendered useless for flying.

PRO ref: AIR 1/1998/204/273/263

The British were able to examine German airfields and hangars after the Armistice on 11 November 1918. They reported that this hangar at Saarbrücken was capable of accommodating thirty machines, had a concrete floor and was well lighted and heated. The doors struck the British as particularly interesting: 'they consisted of corrugated iron strips, all joined and hinged together, which, when opened up, assumed a concertina shape'.

PRO ref: AIR 1/1998/204/273/263

A Zeppelin shed at Mauberge in France, photographed by the RAF on 1 December 1918. Three RFC squadrons were based at this airfield for a few days in August 1914 but it was then occupied by the Germans until the end of the war.

PRO ref: ADM/4125

German airfields became important targets for the RAF in the closing stages of the war, when the British, French and Americans were advancing on the Western Fronts, with close support from the air. This hangar at Nieuwmunster-Houtave airfield, near Bruges, was completely burnt out.

PRO ref: AIR 1/2121/207/56/2

PERFORMING ON THE WORLD STAGE

In 1916 the Signals Experimental Establishment at Woolwich was set up by the War Office to develop wireless and line equipment for the Army. Later its interests were expanded to include development of a wide range of electrical and electronic equipment for military purposes. After the Germans began air raids on Britain, a 'Trumpet Locator' was constructed for picking up approaching aircraft, based on the work of the National Physical Laboratory and the Anti-Aircraft Experimental Section of the Munitions Inventions Department. This photograph, taken on 27 January 1920, showed the device on a projector base, with a trumpet of 39 inches diameter in the telescoped position.

PRO ref: AVIA 23/54

The 'Trumpet Collector' part of the device.
PRO ref: AVIA 23/54

The Women's Royal Air Force (WRAF) was formed at the same time as the RAF on 1 April 1918. It was recruited from volunteers who had served with the air units of the Women's Royal Naval Service (WRNS) and the Women's Auxiliary Army Corps (WAAC), as well as from the Voluntary Aid Detachment (VAD) Corps and the Women's Legion. The women did not serve overseas during the war, but in March 1919, when this photograph was taken, a contingent went to France to replace men eligible for demobilization. Another contingent followed a month later to join the army of occupation in Cologne.

MoD ref: H2332

The *R34* airship, 643 feet long and powered by five Sunbeam Maori engines of 270 hp, was completed by Beardmore in 1919 for the RAF and stationed at Pulham in Norfolk. She was the first lighter-than-air craft to make a transatlantic flight, leaving East Fortune in East Lothian on 2 July 1919 and arriving at Mineola airfield near New York four days later. She left again on 10 July and arrived at Pulham after a flight of 75 hours. Her career ended when she was damaged beyond repair after hitting a hill on 28 January 1921. This photograph was taken when *R34* flew over the Public Record Office in Chancery Lane, London.

PRO ref: PRO 50/59

DH9s made a major contribution to the reputation of the RAF after the First World War, at a time when continued independence from the Army and Navy was in doubt. In January 1920 the Chief of Air Staff, Sir Hugh Trenchard, sent twelve of these aircraft to British Somaliland to help subdue a dissident known as 'The Mad Mullah', who had defied the civil administration since the beginning of the century. These aircraft, known as 'Z Force', bombed the Mullah's emplacements and put him and his followers to flight. The long military campaign was thus ended after only three weeks of air operations, with a minimum of expense. The enemy's positions were then occupied by the Camel Corps and the King's African Rifles. This DH9 of Z Force, serial D3117, was also employed as an air ambulance.

MoD ref: H95

The Fairey Pintail III seaplane, serial N135, which made its maiden flight on 8 November 1921. Only three Pintails were built, of which this was the last.

PRO ref: AIR 5/1363

This prototype Vickers Virginia, serial J6856, first flew at Brooklands on 24 November 1922. The twin-engined night bomber carried a crew of four and equipped several heavy bomber squadrons.

PRO ref: AIR 5/1360

Further experiments with Vickers Virginias were carried out, such as this Mark III serial J7131. Variants of this heavy bomber continued in RAF service until the last machine was withdrawn in February 1938.

MoD ref: H1586

This Vickers Vulture I amphibian flying boat serial G–EBHO, with Napier Lion engines, took off from Calshot seaplane base on 25 March 1924 on a British World Flight sponsored by *The Times*. It was delayed by engine trouble in Corfu but eventually flew via Athens and Cairo to RAF Hinaidi, where it arrived in the afternoon of 20 April.

PRO ref: AIR 23/7386

Dressed formally for the reception at Hinaidi were the organizer and navigator, Squadron Leader A.S.C. Maclaren (left) and the pilot Flying Officer W.N. Plenderleith (right), with the flight engineer Sergeant R. Andrews in the front cockpit. The machine later crashed when taking off from Akyab in Burma during the monsoon. Another machine was brought out from Tokyo by an

American destroyer and the flight continued. However, this replacement came down on 2 August in heavy seas off Siberia when thick fog was encountered. The airmen were not injured but the flying boat was so badly damaged that the flight was abandoned.

PRO ref: AIR 23/7386

The de Havilland 9A, known as the 'Ninak', entered RAF service in June 1918 and then continued in front-line squadrons as a standard day bomber until 1931. It flew on bombing raids over Germany at the end of the First World War, served on the side of White Russians in the war against the revolutionary forces, in home-based squadrons, in the Middle East and in India. The DH9A in this photograph, serial J7832, was on the strength of 45 Squadron, based at Helwan in Egypt in 1928.

MoD ref: H97

The Vickers Vernon was the first aircraft in the RAF to be designed principally as a troop transport. It first entered service with 45 Squadron at Hinaidi in Iraq during March 1922, providing mobility which enabled the Army to control the country with far fewer troops. Vernons of 45 and 70 Squadrons also took over an air mail service between Heliopolis near Cairo and Hinaidi near Baghdad, as shown in this photograph dated 1923 of an aircraft of 70 Squadron. This air mail route had been pioneered in July 1921 by DH9s of 30 and 47 Squadrons, and from the following October RAF aircraft carried civil mail at one shilling an ounce as well as official mail. The air mail service was handed over to Imperial Airways at the end of 1926.

PRO ref: AIR 23/7386

The Secretary of State for Air, Lord Thompson, photographed in front of a Vickers Vernon during a visit to RAF Hinaidi on 26 September 1924. Brigadier-General Christopher B. Thompson was created Baron Thompson of Cardington on 11 February 1924 and was then mainly responsible for a three-year scheme of air development which included the building of the airships *R100* and *R101*. He was killed in the disaster which befell *R101* at Beauvais in France on 5 October 1930.

PRO ref: AIR 23/7386

Avro 504Ns of 601 (County of London) Squadron, which was equipped with these machines about seven months after its formation at Northolt in Middlesex on 14 October 1925 as a light bomber squadron of the Auxiliary Air Force. DH9s arrived in June 1926, but the Avro 504Ns continued as trainers.

MoD ref: H37

The first successful round-the-world flight took place between 4 April and 28 September 1924. Four Douglas World Cruisers took off from Seattle in Washington and flew westwards. Three of these reached RAF Hinaidi in Iraq on 8 July, one of which was photographed when landing.

PRO ref: AIR 23/7386

Douglas World Cruiser *New Orleans*, crewed by Lts. Erik Nelson and John Harding Jr, at RAF Hinaidi.

PRO ref: AIR 23/7386

The three American crews photographed at RAF Hinaidi. Two aircraft completed the round-the-world flight. They were *Chicago*, crewed by Lts. Lowell H. Smith and Leslie P. Arnold, and *New Orleans*, crewed by Lts. Erik Nelson and John Harding Jr.

PRO ref: AIR 23/7386

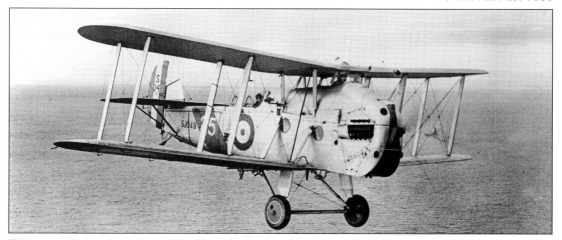

This ungainly aircraft was a Blackburn Blackburn, serial S1049, designed for spotter-reconnaissance duties in the Fleet Air Arm. The Blackburn first entered service in June 1923 with 422 Flight on the carrier HMS *Eagle* in the Mediterranean Fleet, and subsequently equipped other units. The bulky fuselage was built to accommodate an observer and a wireless operator, but its shape did not improve the aircraft's performance. The Blackburn continued until March 1933, when it was replaced with the Fairey IIIF.

MoD ref: H47

A DH9A flying over northern Kurdistan in the vicinity of the Rowandus Valley, around 1925. The aircraft may have been on the strength of either 55 Squadron or 84 Squadron, both of which were based in Iraq during this time as part of the peace-keeping force. The photograph was pasted in a Staff Memoranda folder in order to show the mountainous nature of the country.

PRO ref: AIR 8/72

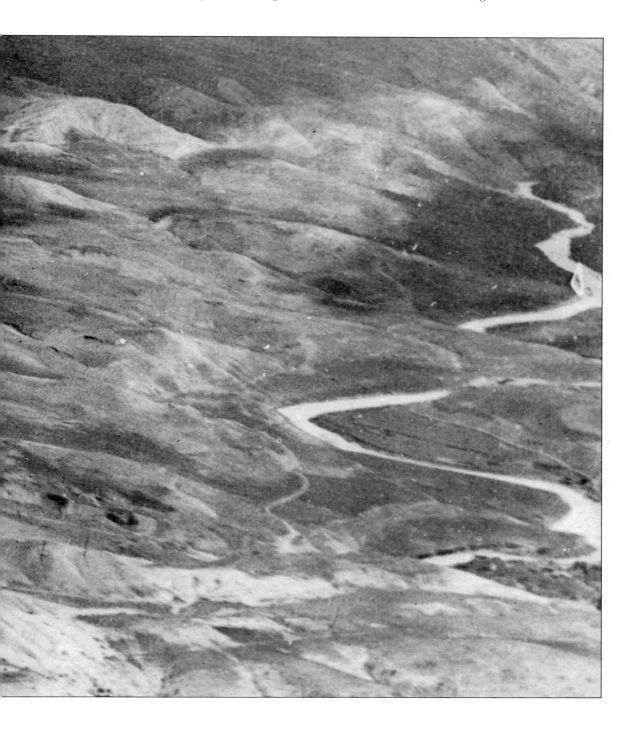

The ancient city of Sammarrah in Iraq, photographed by the RAF in about 1924. According to an Arabian fable, a servant who was frightened by the appearance of Death in the market-place of Baghdad and stole his master's horse to escape to Sammarrah, then found that his true appointment with Death was in this town.

PRO ref: AIR 23/7386

The Avro Bison was a contemporary of the Blackburn Blackburn, and the two companies seem to have vied with each other in producing the ugliest naval aircraft of the period. The pilot looked down the nose of the aircraft at an angle of 45 degrees while two (and sometimes three) air observers and wireless operators worked in a large enclosed compartment behind him. The first Bisons were delivered in March 1923 to the RAF's 3 Squadron, which was disbanded shortly afterwards. Thereafter the machines went to the Fleet Air Arm and continued in service until 1929. This Bison was photographed over Malta.

MoD ref: H1628

This Parnall Peto floatplane, serial N181, was one of two designed for stowage in a hangar on the deck of a submarine. The photograph was taken at Felixstowe in 1925. The aircraft was rebuilt three years later and given the new serial N255. It was lost on 26 January 1932 when HM Submarine *M–2* foundered off Portland in Dorset.

PRO ref: AVIA 19/495

The Supermarine Southampton flying boat entered the RAF in August 1925. Serving at home, Iraq and Singapore, it achieved fame for long-distance flights and continued to give excellent service for over ten years. This Southampton serial S1043 was on the strength of 201 Squadron and remained in service until July 1935.

MoD ref: H329

The Handley Page Hyderabad was a heavy night bomber which first came into service in December 1925 with 99 Squadron at Bircham Newton in Norfolk. Only thirty-eight were built, serving in squadrons at home, the last becoming obsolete in 1934.

MoD ref: H1198

Fairey IIID serial N9451 was the first production aircraft of the version which, in 1920, followed the Fairey IIIC seaplane. It could be fitted with either wheels or floats and was employed as both a reconnaissance and bomber aircraft, serving in the RAF and the Fleet Air Arm. The early Fairey IIID was powered by a Rolls-Royce Eagle engine. Later versions formed the RAF's long-distance flights which made history in 1926.

PRO ref: AIR 5/1363

The first of the long-distance flights to the Cape of Good Hope was made by Fairey IIIDs. It began on 1 March 1926 when four aircraft led by Wing Commander C.W.H. Pulford set off from Heliopolis near Cairo. They reached Cape Town on 19 April and then flew to Lee-on-Solent, where they arrived on 21 June, having flown a distance of 13,901 miles without mechanical failures or mishaps. This Fairey IIID serial S1102 was one of the four aircraft.

MoD ref: H1614

Between June and August 1928 operations were carried out in the Dala area of Aden Protectorate against incursions of forces from the Yemen. When these forces refused to withdraw from their garrisons, bombing and other operations totalling 927 hours were carried out by Fairey IIIFs from RAF Kormaksar. This fort at Dala was one of the main targets. The light bombs made little impression on the walls but their blast was sufficient to scatter the enemy soldiers. Several aircraft were hit by rifle fire and one crashed in a sandstorm. The Yemeni forces evacuated the area on 25 August 1928 and it was then reoccupied by the Protectorate tribesmen.

PRO ref: AIR 5/1299

The Fairey IIIF was an improved version of the Fairey IIID, with cleaner lines and fitted with a Napier Lion XIA engine, which entered RAF service in December 1927. It was a two-seater general-purpose aircraft which gave excellent service both at home and abroad, and also made a

number of notable long-distance flights in Africa. This Fairey IIIF serial S1210, an all-metal Mark II version, was photographed at 2,000 feet over Sliema in Malta on 1 February 1929.

MoD ref: H138

The Saro Valkyrie seaplane, serial N186, was ordered in February 1925. Between 12 August and 28 September 1927 it participated in a goodwill tour of Scandinavian capitals made by the Flying Boat Development Flight, together with a Southampton, an Iris, and a Singapore, on a round trip of 9,400 miles. This photograph was taken at Felixstowe in 1927. Serial N186 was the only Valkyrie built; it was dismantled at Cowes in 1929.

PRO ref: AVIA 19/501

This Cierva C10 autogyro serial J9038, built by Parnall for the RAF, rolled over during taxiing trials carried out by the Royal Aircraft Establishment at Andover in Hampshire on 5 November 1928. The accident was attributed to incorrect setting of the rotor axis.

PRO ref: AVIA 6/1745

Cardington Airship Station under construction on 25 April 1925, at a time when airships were considered to be one of the most important means of transport of the future.

PRO ref: AIR 59/3

Airship mooring mast at Cardington on 22 January 1926.

PRO ref: AIR 59/3

Cardington Airship Station nearing completion on 22 January 1926.

PRO ref: AIR 59/3

The airship *R101*, 777 feet long, attached to her mooring mast at the Royal Airship Works in Cardington. She was ready to fly in October 1929 and, after test flights, left Cardington on 4 October 1930 for Karachi.

PRO ref: AIR 5/919

The verandah of the airship *R101*, reminiscent of an ocean liner, photographed on 18 November 1929.

PRO ref: AIR 59/4

The passenger lounge of the airship *R101*, photographed on 18 November 1929.

PRO ref: AIR 59/4

The dining room of the airship *R101*, fitted with lightweight cane furniture, photographed on 18 November 1929.

PRO ref: AIR 59/4

The wreckage of the airship *R101* after crashing near Beauvais in France on 5 October 1930, while en route to India from Cardington. Only six survived from the fifty-four on board. Among the dead were the Secretary of State for Air, Lord Thompson, and the Director of Civil Aviation, Sir Sefton Brancker.

PRO ref: AIR 5/919

The Hawker Horsley entered service in 1927 as a day bomber and served in home-based squadrons as well as the Far East. These machines, serials S1443, S1604 and S1640, were on the strength of 36 Squadron, which was equipped with Horsleys from October 1928 to July 1935, when based in Britain and then in Singapore and Malaya.

MoD ref: H205

The Vickers Vimy heavy bomber, which came into service too late for the First World War, achieved fame when Capt. John Alcock and Lt. Arthur W. Brown made the first direct crossing of the Atlantic in an adapted machine on 14/15 June 1919. It was employed in Parachute Training Schools from 1928. The trainees clung to struts during take-off and allowed the parachutes to stream out when the Vimy reached sufficient altitude.

MoD ref: H712

Parachutists leaving the Vickers Vimy.

MoD ref: H716

This Armstrong Whitworth Atlas serial J9983 was photographed picking up a message at Hendon in 1929. The two-seater Atlas was introduced into RAF service in October 1927 as the first machine specially designed for army co-operation work. It was also employed on communications work and as an advanced trainer.

MoD ref: H27

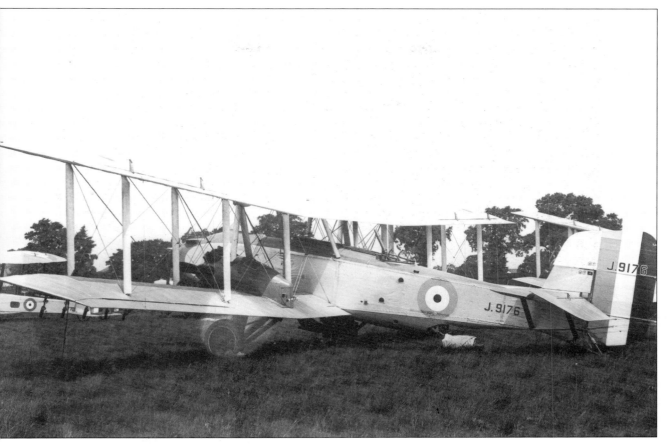

The Boulton & Paul Sidestrand was a twin-engined bomber, with three or four seats, which entered service with only one RAF squadron in March 1929. This was 101 Squadron at Bircham Newton in Norfolk, which was equipped with these aircraft until July 1936. The Sidestrand was designed as a medium bomber and fulfilled this role admirably, but only eighteen were produced, such as serial J9176 in this photograph.

MoD ref: H56

The Hawker Hart came into service in January 1930 as a two-seat light bomber and proved highly successful, its maximum speed of 185 mph being very fast for the era. Harts served at home and in India and Egypt, the last being withdrawn from squadron service in 1939. The Hart in this

photograph was on the strength of 604 (County of Middlesex) Squadron, which was equipped with these machines from September 1934 to June 1935 when based at Hendon.

MoD ref: H1146

The Fairey Flycatcher single-seat fighter served with the Fleet Air Arm from 1923 to 1934. Serial N163 in this photograph was the first of three prototypes, making its maiden flight on 28 November 1922. Flycatchers were unusual since the wings did not fold but could be dismantled easily for stowage on aircraft and capital ships. The flaps extended along the trailing edges of both wings, thus shortening take-off and landing distances. The undercarriage could be interchanged with twin floats or combined wheels and floats.

PRO ref: AIR 5/240

The Fairey Flycatcher serial N9619 over Leuchars in Fifeshire on 7 October 1930. This highly manoeuvrable machine was easy to fly and maintain, but the upswept underside of the fuselage and large wheels presented a rather strange appearance in flight.

MoD ref: H128

Westland Wapiti IIA serial J9728, photographed on 17 September 1930. This two-seat and general-purpose aircraft could be fitted with either a Jupiter VIII engine of 480 hp or a Jupiter FXA of 550 hp. The Mark I version first entered service in July 1938. Many RAF squadrons at home, in Iraq and India were equipped with the reliable Wapiti, which remained in service until 1939. The Wapiti in this photograph was a research and development machine used by both the Royal Aircraft Establishment at Farnborough and the Aeroplane and Armament Experimental Establishment at Boscombe Down. It made its last flight at Farnborough in July 1935.

PRO ref: AIR 2/790

The Fairey Gordon was a development of the Fairey IIIF, with an improved performance, which first entered RAF service in April 1931. It served at home and abroad, continuing in overseas squadrons until the outbreak of the Second World War. This Fairey Gordon serial K2645 of

47 Squadron was photographed over Jebel Kassala in the Sudan, at a time when the squadron was based at Khartoum. It lasted until 31 May 1939 when it crashed on landing at Habbaniya in Iraq.

MoD ref: H150

The Short Rangoon flying boat equipped two RAF squadrons, only six being built. These machines were delivered from April 1931 to 203 Squadron at Basrah in Iraq, where they were employed on anti-smuggling patrols over the Persian Gulf. They began to return to England in September 1935 and were taken on charge by 210 Squadron, based at Pembroke Dock and then at

Gibraltar, before being replaced in August 1936. The aircraft in this photograph, serial S1433, joined Imperial Airways in September 1936 as G–AEIM and was used as a crew trainer until 1938.

MoD ref: H1705

Supermarine S6B serial S1595, the high-speed seaplane which was flown by Ft. Lt. J.N. Boothman to win first place in the twelfth Schneider Trophy contest held on the Solent on 12 September 1931. This gave the RAF its third successive win in the competition, thus gaining the trophy in perpetuity. On 29 September 1931 this machine was flown by Flt. Lt. G.H. Stainforth at 407.5 mph to give Britain the World Speed Record. The experience gained with Supermarine racing seaplanes had an important influence on the design of the Spitfire. The seaplane in this photograph is now on display at the Science Museum in London.

PRO ref: INF 2/3

This Fairey long-range monoplane serial K1991, fitted with a Napier Lion XIA engine of 570 hp, was the second built in an attempt to achieve a long-distance record for Great Britain. The first machine, serial J9479, hit high ground south of Tunis on 16 December 1929, killing the crew. K1991 made two attempts. On the second occasion, with Sqn. Ldr. O.R. Gayford as pilot and Flt. Lt. G.E. Nicholetts as navigator, the monoplane took off from Harwell in Berkshire on 6 February 1933 and created a record by arriving in Walvis Bay in south-west Africa after 57 hours 25 minutes. This photograph was taken when it returned to Farnborough on 2 May 1933.

MoD ref: H165

In front of the Fairey long-range monoplane at Farnborough. Left to right: Flt. Lt. G.E. Nicholetts, Lord Londonderry (Secretary of State for Air), Sqn. Ldr. O.R. Gayford, Air Chief Marshal Sir John Salmond (Chief of Air Staff).

MoD ref: H168

The Hawker Audax two-seater first appeared in 1931 as a replacement for the Armstrong Whitworth Atlas on army co-operation duties. It also served as a trainer up to 1941. This Audax serial K3079 was on the strength of 4 Squadron, which was equipped with these machines from December 1931 to July 1937, when based at Farnborough and then Odiham.

MoD ref: H227

144

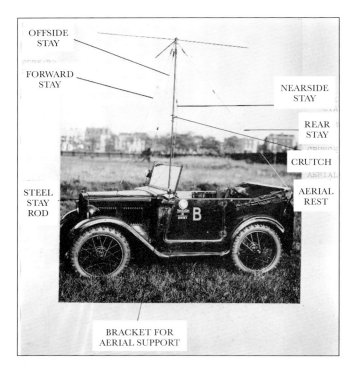

OFFSIDE STAY

FORWARD STAY

NEARSIDE STAY

REAR STAY

CRUTCH

STEEL STAY ROD

AERIAL REST

BRACKET FOR AERIAL SUPPORT

A 1931 Austin 7 chassis adapted to fit the RAF's No. 1 Wireless Set, giving a two-seater mobile unit.

PRO ref: AVIA 23/542

The de Havilland Tiger Moth, a two-seat *ab initio* trainer, was first introduced into RAF service in 1932 and continued with Elementary Flying Training Schools for over fifteen years. It was a very stable aircraft to fly and many former RAF pilots look back on the machine with much affection. This example, serial K2579, was part of the original production batch.

PRO ref: SUPP 9/1

RAF armoured cars worked in collaboration with RAF aircraft in maintaining control over vast areas of the Middle East which were part of the British Empire between the wars. This armoured car, with an RAF roundel on its turret, was named 'Cerberus', the mythical dog which guarded the entrance to Hades. The crew had stopped for a meal, a 'brew-up' of tea from a water tank, and a smoke.

MoD ref: H496

The Vickers Vildebeest was a torpedo-bomber which entered RAF service in November 1932. It was a slow but reliable aircraft which was eventually replaced in the UK by the Bristol Beaufort monoplane after the outbreak of the Second World War. Nevertheless two RAF squadrons, based in Singapore and equipped with these obsolete biplanes, fought against the Japanese when they

invaded Malaya in December 1941. One of these was 100 Squadron, photographed here at Kuala Lumpur in 1938. Many of the aircraft were lost in these engagements.

MoD ref: H368

RAF armoured cars on operations against a dissident Sheik in Iraq. These machines were adapted from the world-famous Silver Ghost cars manufactured by Rolls-Royce.

MoD ref: H1062

On 1 May 1933 the Italian Government held a ceremonial funeral in Florence for Sqn. Ldr. Herbert J.L. Hinkler AFC DSM. Bert Hinkler, who had achieved a number of air records, took off in Puss Moth CF–APK from Lympne in Kent on 7 January 1933 in an attempt to beat the World Speed Record to his native Australia. An extensive search took place when he disappeared, in the belief that he had crashed in the Alps, but his body and aircraft were eventually found in the remote region of Piano della Vache in the Etruscan Apennines, near Arezzo.

PRO ref: AVIA 2/606

The Saro Cloud was an amphibian aircraft, which in August 1933 entered service with the Seaplane Training Squadron at Calshot in Hampshire. It also saw service with the School of Air Pilotage at Andover in Hampshire. The only squadron to be equipped with Saro Clouds was 48 Squadron at Manston in Kent, from February to June 1936. This aircraft, serial K3726, was photographed at Calshot.

MoD ref: H1887

The prototype of the Westland Wallace, serial K3488, was photographed on 9 March 1934. It was built from two airframes of its predecessor, the Westland Wapiti, but fitted with a more powerful Bristol Pegasus engine of 680 hp. It was a general-purpose machine with two seats.

PRO ref: AIR 2/790

The canopy of the Westland Wallace, which could be folded back in sections, was a luxury in the days of open cockpits. This prototype, which was originally known as the Wapiti VII or the PV6, crashed on 13 December 1935.

PRO ref: AIR 2/790

This Westland Wallace, serial K3562, was fitted with four 112 lb bombs. Three home-based squadrons were equipped with Wallaces.

MoD ref: H1815

This prototype of the de Havilland Dominie, DH89M (serial K4772), was photographed in May 1935. It was adapted from the de Havilland Rapide light airliner for the RAF's general reconnaissance duties but was rejected in favour of the Avro Anson. However, it was used for training wireless operators from September 1939, being given the name Dominie in January 1941. Serial K4772 remained in service until July 1942.

PRO ref: AIR 2/1511

The Supermarine Walrus, an amphibian flying boat with a pusher engine, first came into service with the RAF in 1935 but was also used by the Fleet Air Arm. It was rather indecorously nicknamed 'The Shagbat' but nevertheless was regarded with great affection, particularly for its role during the Second World War in air-sea rescue at home and abroad. The Walrus in this photograph, serial K5773, was the second produced from the Air Ministry's first contract.

PRO ref: SUPP 9/1

The prototype of the Avro Anson, serial K4771, was a military version of the Avro 652A commercial aircraft. This photograph was taken in May 1935 after the aircraft had made its first flight on 24 March 1935. It was chosen for reconnaissance duties with Coastal Command but continued in numerous roles with the RAF until 1968. Known as the highly reliable 'Faithful Annie', it was regarded with affection by many RAF trainees, who will doubtless remember that the undercarriage was cranked up by 122 turns of a handle, thus improving their physical fitness.

PRO ref: AIR 2/1511

The first Hawker Hinds entered squadron service in December 1935 and were employed as day bombers. They continued for the next four years, by which time they had given way to new monoplane bombers. This Hind serial K5401 was on the strength of 44 Squadron, which was re-formed at Wyton in Huntingdonshire in March 1937.

MoD ref: H975

The single-seat Bristol Bulldog entered service in May 1929 and remained one of the most popular RAF fighters until 1936, employed mostly on home defence. It was armed with two Vickers guns firing through the propeller and could also carry a light load of four 20 lb bombs. These Bulldog IIAs were on the strength of 54 Squadron, which was equipped with these machines from April 1930 to September 1936, based for most of this period at Hornchurch in Essex.

MoD ref: H752

The sad end of two Westland Wapiti IIAs of 5 Squadron at Quetta in India in February 1934, when the pilot of one attempted to take off over another which had just landed.

MoD ref: H1222

Hawker Harts of 39 Squadron, photographed at Miramshah in Waziristan, India, in 1938. The squadron continued with these machines until August 1939, when it was re-equipped with Bristol Blenheim Is at Tengah in Singapore.

MoD ref: H214

The first royal review of the RAF took place on 6 July 1935, when King George V visited Mildenhall in Suffolk in the year of the Silver Jubilee of his accession to the throne. Thirty-seven squadrons and one composite unit, totalling 356 aircraft, were drawn up in a semi-circle, including the Handley Page Heyfords in this photograph. In the afternoon there was a fly-past at Duxford in Cambridgeshire.

MoD ref: H1548

Three kings in RAF uniform. Left to right: the Prince of Wales (later King Edward VIII); King George V; the Duke of York (later King George VI).

MoD ref: H483

The Hawker Hardy, a two-seater used for general-purpose duties, first entered service in April 1935. Only three squadrons were equipped with this machine, all overseas. This Hardy serial K4053 of 30 Squadron was photographed at Mosul in Iraq in 1935, being guarded by No. 8 Company Kurdish Levies. A few of these aircraft continued in service until 1941.

MoD ref: H923

THE STORM CLOUDS GATHER

In spring 1937 a flight of Vickers Valentia Is of 70 Squadron were sent from their base at Hinaidi in Iraq to Miramshah in Waziristan, India, to help in the evacuation of wounded after an insurrection had broken out. In this photograph Sikh soldiers are loading stretcher cases into Valentia I serial K2340.

PRO ref: AIR 2/2758

The Vickers Wellesley, which entered RAF service in April 1937 as a two-seat bomber, achieved fame for breaking the World Long-distance Record. On 5 November three Wellesleys, led by Sqn. Ldr. R. Kellett, took off from Ismailia in Egypt, and two of these reached Darwin in Australia after flying non-stop for a distance of 7,162 miles. This Wellesley I serial L2654 of 14 Squadron was photographed in 1938 over RAF Amman in Jordan.

MoD ref: H373

The Hawker Hector was the last of the Hawker biplanes to enter service with the RAF at home, in May 1937. Like its predecessors, it was a two-seater employed on army co-operation, but it was fitted with a Napier Dagger engine instead of the Rolls-Royce Kestrels of the earlier Hawker biplanes. Some Hectors remained with RAF Auxiliary Squadrons until 1940 and a few even made dive-bombing attacks against German troops in May 1940.

MoD ref: H1375

Problems occurred during the summer of 1937 in the district of Wadi Ma'adin, about 50 miles north-west of Aden, when tribesmen began waylaying motor vehicles and extracting money from their occupants. With the authority of the local Sultan, a column of the Lahej Trained Forces entered the area and demanded that the village chiefs answer to charges brought against them. All but one chief submitted, and warnings were given to evacuate his village. On 22 September 1937 practice bombs were dropped on the outskirts of the village by Vickers Vincents of 8 Squadron based at Khormaksaz. When it seemed that all inhabitants had left, six aircraft in two flights dropped 20 lb bombs in the fields around the village, as shown in this photograph taken from 2,000 feet. It was reported that the area became peaceful after this operation.

PRO ref: AIR 5/1299

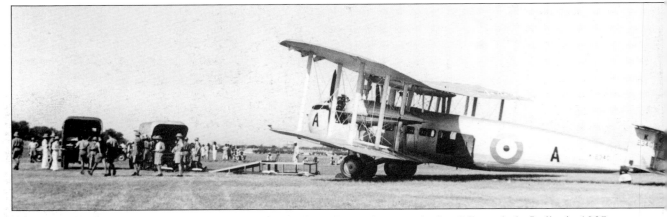

This Vickers Valentia I serial K2340 of 70 Squadron, photographed at Miramshah, India, in 1937, was originally the prototype for the Vickers Victoria V but was rebuilt as a Valentia. These machines served in the Middle East and India, first entering squadron service in September 1935. They proved ideal for transport work over remote terrains but could also carry a bomb load of up to 2,200 lb. Some Valentias continued on communication work until as late as November 1944.

PRO ref: AIR 2/2758

An air gunner of 23 Squadron, wearing his flying suit, parachute, helmet and intercommunication cord, standing beside the rear cockpit of a Hawker Demon in 1937. The Demon two-seat fighter, adapted from the Hart, entered service in March 1931. From October 1936 all Demons were fitted with a Fraser-Nash hydraulic turret armed with a single Lewis gun and spare pans of ammunition, as shown in this photograph.

MoD ref: H909

Troops wearing tropical kit and Wolsley helmets, with their packs squared up and carrying Lee Enfield .303 inch rifles at the trail, emplaning in a Vickers Victoria, ominously labelled 'Mayfly', in 1938.

MoD ref: H345

This prototype of the Hawker Hurricane I, serial K5083, made its maiden flight on 6 November 1935 and proved an immediate success. Production Hurricane Is, with Rolls-Royce Merlin II engines of 1,030 hp and eight machine-guns in the wings, entered RAF service in December 1937. The machine was a rugged and reliable interceptor which later bore the brunt of the fighting in the Battle of France and the Battle of Britain. Variants of the Hurricane continued in front-line service until January 1947.

MoD ref: H245

This prototype of the Fairey Battle, serial K4303, first flew on 10 March 1936 and was intended to supply the RAF with a three-seater monoplane for tactical bombing duties. Battles first entered front-line service in May 1937 and several squadrons that formed part of the Advanced Air Striking Force, which went to France in September 1939, were equipped with these machines. They proved no match for German fighters, being too slow and inadequately equipped with defensive armament. After the fall of France, most of the survivors were turned over to training duties.

MoD ref: H177

The Gloster Gladiator was the last of the RAF's single-seat biplane fighters. Fitted with four forward-firing machine-guns, it entered squadron service in February 1937. Although most were superseded by monoplane fighters at home when the Second World War broke out, Gladiators fought in the Battle of France and one squadron was still equipped with these machines during the

Battle of Britain. Overseas, Gladiators acquitted themselves well in the initial defence of Malta, in
Greece and in the Middle East. These Gladiators were photographed at Ismailia in Egypt in 1938.
MoD ref: H186

A posed photograph of an air observer with an F24 camera. This camera was first introduced in 1925 and remained in RAF service for thirty years. It could be either hand-held or installed in vertical and oblique positions in aircraft. It gave a 5 inch by 5 inch picture and the magazine contained a roll of film which provided up to 125 exposures. Although excellent for low or medium level work, the F24 was not ideal for high-altitude photography. The older F8, with lenses of longer focal length, was employed for high altitude, and the F52 entered service for this purpose in early 1942.

PRO ref: CN 11/6

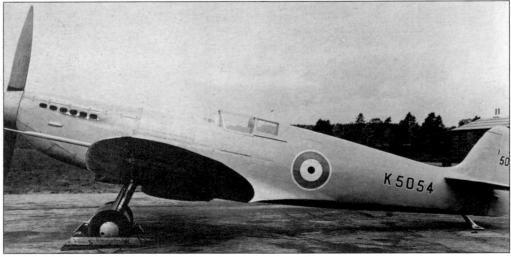

The prototype of the Supermarine Spitfire, serial K5054, made its maiden flight on 4 March 1936. Designed by R.J. Mitchell as a successor to his racing seaplane which won the Schneider Trophy for Great Britain in 1931, it was immediately recognized as a superb fighter with an astonishing performance. Fitted with a Rolls-Royce Merlin engine of 1,030 hp and eight machine-guns in its wings, the Spitfire I entered squadron service in June 1938 and thereafter this beautiful machine and its variants achieved undying world fame.

MoD ref: H334

This prototype of the Armstrong Whitworth Whitley, serial K4586, was designed as a night bomber and made its maiden flight on 17 March 1936. The Whitley I first entered RAF service in March 1937. Together with later variants, including the Mark III with a ventral 'dustbin' turret which could be lowered from the fuselage, the Whitley became one of Bomber Command's main heavy bombers in the early years of the Second World War. Squadrons equipped with these machines were engaged on dropping propaganda leaflets over Germany during the 'Phoney War' before May 1940, with little effect on the population but at the cost of quite heavy losses.

MoD ref: H31

This prototype of the Vickers Wellington, serial K4049, made its maiden flight on 15 June 1936 at Brooklands, near Weybridge in Surrey. Its ingenious geodetic frame was covered with fabric skinning, a construction which later proved capable of absorbing considerable punishment from flak. The prototype was destroyed in an accident on 17 April 1937 but the production Wellington Mark I, powered by two Bristol Pegasus engines and fitted with power-operated turrets in nose, tail and ventral positions, incorporated several improvements to the fuselage and fin. The Mark I entered squadron service in October 1938 and variants of this highly successful aircraft flew throughout the Second World War.

MoD ref: H394

This prototype of the Bristol Blenheim I, serial K7033, first flew on 25 June 1936 and was acclaimed as a very fast bomber for that period. Production Blenheim Is entered squadron service in March 1937. Superseded by the Blenheim IV in home-based squadrons before the outbreak of the Second World War, the Mark I continued to serve in overseas squadrons.

PRO ref: SUPP 9/1

This Handley Page Hampden I serial L4033 was the second aircraft in the first production run, tested at Boscombe Down in Wiltshire on 6 May 1938. The prototype Hampden, serial K4240, first flew on 21 June 1936. RAF squadrons began to receive Hampdens in August 1938, a year before the start of the Second World War. Although more manoeuvrable than its contemporaries, the Hampden was not fitted with power-operated turrets and its defensive armament proved inadequate for the daylight operations on which it was first employed.

PRO ref: AVIA 18/684

The Westland Lysander I was the first monoplane to enter service with the RAF's army co-operation squadrons when it arrived in 16 Squadron at Old Sarum in Wiltshire during May 1938. Nicknamed the 'Lizzie', it was a two-seater employed mainly on artillery spotting and reconnaissance but could also carry light bombs. This example, serial L4729, was one of the first production batch of 144 aircraft.

PRO ref: SUPP 9/1

This prototype of the Short Sunderland I, serial K4774, made its maiden flight on 16 October 1937 and production aircraft entered squadron service in June of the following year. Employed with Coastal Command at home and maritime squadrons abroad, the four-engined Sunderland flying boat became one of the most successful and long-serving aircraft in the RAF, the last being finally retired from front-line duties at Seletar, Singapore, in May 1959.

PRO ref: SUPP 9/1

The Westland Whirlwind was the first twin-engined fighter to enter service with the RAF, the prototype being flown in October 1938. It was fitted with four 20 mm cannon in the nose. Whirlwinds did not enter squadron service until December 1940 and proved effective at low level, especially as escorts on daylight raids. This photograph of the second prototype, serial L6845, was taken in July 1940 at the Aeroplane and Armament Experimental Establishment at Boscombe Down in Wiltshire. The aircraft flew later with 263 Squadron, which was equipped with these machines from July 1940 to December 1943, but struck some trees at Llandenny near Usk on 11 June 1941, when the squadron was based at Filton in Gloucestershire. Only 112 Whirlwinds were built.

PRO ref: AVIA 18/691

This Bristol Beaufort I torpedo-bomber, serial L4442, was the second prototype and first flew in July 1939. The machine was fitted with Bristol Taurus VI engines of 1,130 hp and was difficult to fly on one engine. Production aircraft first entered service with Coastal Command in November 1939. Teething problems were gradually overcome but the squadrons suffered severe casualties, primarily owing to the nature of the operations on which they were employed.

PRO ref: SUPP 9/1

The Short Stirling I was the first four-engined monoplane to enter service with Bomber Command. Designed by the company which had specialized in flying boats, this prototype, serial L7600, first flew on 14 May 1939 but crashed on landing and was destroyed. However, Stirlings entered squadron service in August 1940 and continued in the bomber role until 1944, although their operational ceiling was lower than that of the Lancaster and the division of the bomb bay into compartments prevented them carrying bombs heavier than 4,000 lb. After withdrawal from bombing, Stirlings carried out special duties such as radar counter-measures, dropping of supplies to Resistance forces, and towing gliders.

PRO ref: SUPP 9/1

A panoramic photograph of the Russian oil refineries at Baku in the Caucasus, taken from the ground for intelligence purposes in 1939. At the time, Russia was supplying Germany with oil and plans were made for the bombing of this target by the RAF from Iraq and the French Air Force from Syria. A spy flight was made by the RAF on 30 March 1940 from Habbaniya, in a Lockheed 14 with civilian markings, and photographs were taken. The Anglo-French plan of attack was abandoned when the German Blitzkrieg was launched in May 1940.

PRO ref: AIR 9/138

INDEX